A SENSE OF BELONGING

Cover: Design by John Chandler using fragments of photographs by Jim Lowe of J & S Photography, Melksham

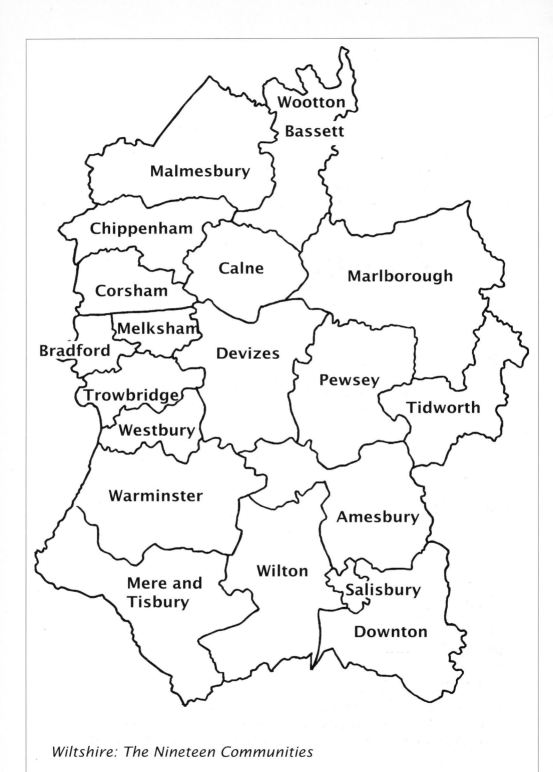

Wiltshire: The Nineteen Communities

A Sense of
Belonging

History, Community,
and the New Wiltshire

John Chandler

EX LIBRIS PRESS
in co-operation with **Wiltshire County Council, Kennet District Council,
North Wiltshire District Council, Salisbury District Council,
West Wiltshire District Council and Wiltshire Health Authority**

Published in 1998 by
EX LIBRIS PRESS
1 The Shambles
Bradford on Avon
Wiltshire
BA15 1JS

Design and Typesetting by Ex Libris Press

Cover printed by Shires Press, Trowbridge
Printed and bound by Cromwell Press, Trowbridge

ISBN 0 948578 93 9

CONTENTS

PREFACE

THIS YEAR I have the privilege of serving as the Chairman of Wiltshire County Council, and am very pleased that we are co-operating with Ex Libris Press in publishing this book. It sums up the history of our County as a whole and gives an introduction to the diversity to be found within the Wiltshire boundary. Each of the nineteen community areas to be found in this book has its own distinct character.

The County Council has been supported in the task of feeding information into this book by a number of our key partners who share our objectives of providing good quality and community based services to Wiltshire's communities. In this respect I would like to mention in particular our four District Councils: Kennet, North Wiltshire, Salisbury, West Wiltshire; and the Wiltshire Health Authority, all of whom have provided information for this book.

The County Council has recently consulted on its Corporate Strategy for the next five years. Our Statement of Purpose is: 'To enhance the opportunities and quality of life of all people living and working in Wiltshire'. There are three tiers of elected local government in a shire county like Wiltshire – the County Council, the four District Councils and the 252 Parish and Town Councils. All these Councils agreed in 1997 a set of principles and policies to work jointly for the benefit of Wiltshire.

The Wiltshire local authorities in the future wish to involve Wiltshire communities to a greater extent, and to have more consultation and local participation. All the councils are committed: to take action at the most 'local' level possible; to seek common boundaries for working together in localities; and to value and respect local diversity.

Over the years a great deal of work has taken place by the different authorities in Wiltshire. Each authority has had ideas about the need in their area. I believe that together we now have a vision for Wiltshire, and that together we can put that vision into action. Action without vision can be disjointed; vision without action is almost useless. I look forward to authorities working within community areas putting the vision and hopes we all have for our County into action. Readers living in Wiltshire will be able to judge, over time, our degree of success in achieving this aim.

John Chandler's book will spread a wider understanding of the diverse nature of Wiltshire. Each of Wiltshire's nineteen community areas is different in significant ways. I represent a Trowbridge division in the County Council. My year of office has shown the level of affection people have for Wiltshire throughout the county. At the same time, people, including councillors, are working hard on projects to improve their local area for the benefit of their community. In my experience this is true from Malmesbury in the north of the county to Downton in the south and from Bradford on Avon in the west to Tidworth and Ludgershall in the east.

I do hope that you enjoy reading about the story of Wiltshire and its communities so admirably told by John Chandler in this book. I am sure that it will tempt you to explore the county and perhaps find out more about your own community area.

Mrs. Grace Hill
Chairman of Wiltshire County Council 1997/98

INTRODUCTION

WHEN I RECEIVED my first payslip from Wiltshire County Council in 1974, local government had just been placed on a new footing. We were all adjusting to changed responsibilities, reshuffled colleagues, and unfamiliar methods of working. Such alterations to the way in which Wiltshire is administered have occurred periodically throughout the nineteenth and twentieth centuries as functions, circumstances, and attitudes have changed.

In 1992 the process of local government reorganization throughout England and Wales began again. There were the usual entrenched loyalties and rivalries, as no fewer than ten options for Wiltshire's future administration were debated in front of a Local Government Commission set up to undertake the review. The principal outcome, implemented in April 1997, was that the Swindon area became self-governing, as a unitary authority, while the rest of Wiltshire continued with two tiers of local government (above parish level) – a new county council, and the four existing district councils, Kennet, Salisbury, North and West Wiltshire.

This was a fundamental change – the first significant redefining of what we mean by Wiltshire as an administrative entity for over a thousand years. But it was not the Review's only achievement. For a decade or more there has been a growing feeling that local government generally should become less monolithic, and more responsive to the varying needs of individual communities. One of the stated aims of the Local Government Review was to create authorities that, 'reflect the identities and interests of local communities', and are based on 'natural communities'. Defining our 'natural communities', and then focusing local service provision on their areas, has become an important element in the restructuring of the new Wiltshire. The idea has been embraced not only by the county and district councils, but also by other organizations which provide local services, such as the police and the health authority. As a result it is intended that an increasing range of contacts and services should in future be provided in each of the nineteen community areas.

But how do we define 'natural communities', and how have we arrived at Wiltshire's nineteen community areas? Most of us probably feel an affinity with the town or village where we live, but how far does that affinity extend? Which villages identify with which towns, and why? And why do some neighbouring towns seem to co-operate, while others compete with each other? Are there unmapped and intangible boundaries running along the countryside, which to cross means passing, for instance, from south to west Wiltshire, or from the Marlborough to the Devizes area?

Of course, in such subjective matters there will never be a consensus, because our individual circumstances affect how we view our surroundings, and how closely we feel bound within a community, large or small. We may, for some of the activities of life, feel part of our village (Corsley, for instance); whereas to a stranger we would say that we came from Warminster, or west Wiltshire; but for work, shopping, and entertainment we might look to Bath. Many Wiltshire villagers identify, in fact, with nearby towns which are not themselves in Wiltshire. And we all, to some extent, depend on the large urban centres – Swindon, Southampton, Bath and Bristol – which lie beyond the boundaries of the new Wiltshire.

Nevertheless, if the concept of communities, especially 'natural communities', is to have any meaning, it must be important to try to define them, and to draw tentative boundaries around them. Some of the criteria for deciding on the extent of community areas are quite self-evident. Geology and the shape of the land may erect barriers, such as tracts of downland and forest. Major roads and railways provide links. Ease of access to a local town, and the range of services it provides, determines the size of its hinterland, the villages and hamlets which depend upon it. Reading the same local newspaper, friendships forged during schooldays, membership of clubs and common interests, where we shop and where we work – these are all elements in the formation of communities.

Although most of us enjoy far greater mobility than our grandparents could have imagined, it is the contention of this book that the communities with which we identify are not, by and large, products of modern living, but have evolved over many centuries. This was recognized during the Local Government Review, which urged participants to take account of the historical basis of their proposed communities. In consequence Wiltshire County Council decided to commission an independent report, 'The History of Wiltshire and its Communities', to explore and address all the historical dimensions of the review. The report was completed in November 1993, and became part of the Council's submission. And it has been used subsequently to help frame policy regarding community focus in Wiltshire. This book is an expansion and reworking of my 1993 report. It is divided into four chapters.

In *A Sense of History* I explore the origins of Wiltshire itself, and the ancient divisions within it; its landscape, agriculture and settlement patterns; the ways in which people have felt allegiance to it, and the various methods of governing it. I look, too, at how towns have emerged as local centres, including the rapid growth of Swindon, and consider how general issues of locality, settlement, and central places have been studied by geographers and historians. *A Sense of Community* is concerned with the various sources of statistical information about Wiltshire and its inhabitants which are available to local government and other authorities, so that they can plan and provide services at community level as effectively as possible. Then, in *Wiltshire Communities*, each of Wiltshire's nineteen community areas is placed under scrutiny. I examine their physical and demographic make-up using the historical and statistical information described in the earlier chapters, and I assess the validity of their boundaries. Finally, in *Belonging in a Community*, the progress so far of Wiltshire's community focus initiative is described, and the opportunities for its future development.

This book has been published in conjunction with, and with encouragement from, Wiltshire County Council, the four district councils, the health authority, and other participating organizations, in order to help to explain and promote Wiltshire's community focus initiative, and to place it in its historical perspective. It is, nevertheless, the work of an individual who has for many years been independent of all these organizations, and who takes sole responsibility for the views and assertions, prejudices and inaccuracies, which it contains. Statements made within it should not be regarded as official policy.

John Chandler
East Knoyle
January 1998

1 A Sense of History

How Old is Wiltshire?

BEFORE ENGLAND had a national identity our country belonged to separate warring kingdoms, whose lands fluctuated, but in due course corresponded roughly to the modern English regions. The kingdom of Wessex controlled the West Country, and during the ninth century extended its domain eastwards across the whole of Southern England south of the Thames. To its north, beyond the Thames and stretching across the Midlands, lay the kingdom of Mercia, enemy territory which included Gloucestershire. The kingdoms of Wessex and Mercia emerged during the Saxon colonization of England in the sixth century, and remained separate until the end of the ninth century. By then Wessex under Alfred had become dominant, and the kingdoms united to fight a common enemy, the Danes.

In order to administer these Saxon kingdoms, they were divided into territories known as shires, which were governed by chieftains known as aldermen, and later by sheriffs (shire-reeves). Wiltshire emerged as one of the six principal shires of Wessex, and was surrounded on most sides by others, the friendly and still familiar Hampshire, Berkshire, Dorsetshire, and Somersetshire. But Wiltshire's northern boundary until Alfred's reign was also the frontier of the kingdom, and so was threatened by the hostile Mercians of Gloucestershire and much fought over. Gains and losses at war may explain the ragged and untidy modern county boundary along the now peaceful Thames Valley north of Cricklade.

The first reference to what may be Wiltshire occurs in the Saxon chronicle against the year 802, when it was called *Wilsaete*, and later in the ninth century the name was spelled *Wiltunscir*. It is very likely that a shire based on Wilton or the Wylye Valley (as the names suggest) existed earlier than this, by about 750 or even 700. But there is no way of knowing what were its boundaries, nor how much of it coincided with medieval and modern Wiltshire. Parts of our modern boundary which follow either ancient earthworks, such as Grim's Ditch on Cranborne Chase, or dense woodland, such as Selwood Forest, may have been in place by 700. Some of North Wiltshire, on the other hand, north of the Wansdyke which crosses the Marlborough Downs, were perhaps once part of Berkshire, and so our north-eastern county boundary may have been decided rather later.

By about the year 900, if not before, Wiltshire's external boundary was settled, and thereafter (although no maps exist until centuries later) we know that it changed hardly at all until anomalies were tidied up by the Victorians. Evidence for this stability comes in the form of taxation records (from Domesday Book onwards), and from the documents and lists created by county administration during the middle ages and later. The first county map was published in 1576.

The attempts to 'tidy-up' which took place, first in 1844, and then during the 1880s and 1890s, and in 1930, mainly concerned places around the edge of Wiltshire, and were all on a small scale. Some involved 'detached' parishes such as Minety, which had been part of Gloucestershire although surrounded by Wiltshire; or Poulton near Cirencester, formerly Wiltshire but surrounded by Gloucestershire. A few Wiltshire parishes near Reading were transferred to Berkshire where, geographically, they had always belonged. Other changes were made to end the inconvenience of communities which were divided between two counties, and Wiltshire also lost small groups of Cotswold parishes to Gloucestershire, and Cranborne Chase parishes to Hampshire. In 1974, when many counties underwent ruthless change and division, Wiltshire was unusual in that its external boundary remained the same. Swindon's long-cherished independence from the rest of Wiltshire, achieved when the former district of Thamesdown Borough became a unitary authority (Swindon Borough Council) in 1997, was the first major alteration to Wiltshire's administrative boundary since Saxon times.

But to trace the origin of our shire and its subsequent boundary changes only takes us part of the way to answering the question, 'How old is Wiltshire?'. Wiltshire as an interlocking series of ancient landscapes, rich in archaeological remains, is obviously a great deal older than the Saxon administrators. And not only the prehistoric monuments and Roman roads, but also some of the boundaries with which this study is concerned, can be shown to be much older than the creation of the shire.

A glance at any of the parish maps in this book reveals that, while many parishes have odd and irregular boundaries, there is a tendency in parts of the county, particularly the chalklands in the south and east, for parishes to be long, narrow strips. Parishes, as we shall see, were created in the early middle ages, and some have later been amalgamated or divided; but their boundaries very often follow precisely the line of older territories, which were described in great detail by documents recording Saxon land transactions. So, underlying the division of Wiltshire into ecclesiastical and modern civil parishes, there is an earlier system of boundaries.

Some of the parish boundaries which we know or suspect to be ancient do quite surprising things. Running north from Pewsey Vale a number of parishes extend up the hillside on to the Marlborough Downs, where they meet others running south from the Kennet Valley. Across the downland runs the massive defensive earthwork of Wansdyke, which can be dated on archaeological grounds to the end of the Roman period, the fourth or early fifth century. Most of the boundaries (such as Stanton St Bernard, Alton Barnes and Priors, and West Overton) choose to ignore it, and extend a little way beyond it, even though it is such a prominent and obviously defining landmark. It appears, therefore, that these boundaries existed before the earthwork, which means that they were laid out during the Roman period, or even earlier. In East Wiltshire the ancient boundary between Chute and Hippenscombe ignores an adjacent Roman road, and so may pre-date it. In recent years many studies have been undertaken into the antiquity of boundaries, and it no longer seems unreasonable that some (although by no means all) of our modern administrative boundaries owe their origins to the peoples of Iron Age or Roman Britain. And because stretches of the external county boundary coincide with what may be very ancient territorial boundaries, parts of it, too, may be much older than the Saxon shire which it encircles.

The small territories, underlying and sometimes pre-dating the formation of parishes, were known as tithings, so-called because at one time, it appears, they were each reckoned for administrative or taxation purposes to comprise ten households. Tithings seem to have been grouped into blocks of ten, known as hundreds, and these hundreds, of which there were about forty in Wiltshire, continued as important units of administration throughout the middle ages, as we shall see. By the time of Domesday Book (1086), when we can first reconstruct the hundreds and their constituent tithings, centuries of modification and reassessment had already blurred and confused whatever had been their original arrangement; but it is striking how many Domesday estates were still being assessed on the basis of ten households, or a multiple of ten.

If a number of the tithing boundaries existed during the Roman period, then we are faced with two further possibilities. One is that some tithings are continuations of estates based on Roman villas - examples might be Box, Bradford on Avon, Lacock, and Atworth. The second is that the grouping of tithings into larger units, the hundreds, might bear some relationship to the territories which were established around the small Roman towns of Wiltshire. Two of Wiltshire's four Roman towns were *Verlucio*, near Sandy Lane, and *Cunetio*, near Mildenhall. It has been noticed that the four hundreds of Calne, Chippenham, Melksham and Cannings, all meet close to the site of *Verlucio*, and that Ramsbury, Selkley and Kinwardstone hundreds meet near the site of *Cunetio*. Perhaps, therefore, they offer a clue to the extent of the Roman towns' territories, which were later divided into hundreds.

When considering the antiquity of boundaries and land divisions we are dealing with civilizations which have left us no accurate maps. Any conclusions we reach, therefore, must be hedged around by uncertainty. With this in mind the answer to our question, 'How old is Wiltshire?', must be that, as a shire, Wiltshire can be traced back to the eighth century, perhaps slightly earlier or slightly later. But we should add that some of Wiltshire's internal and external boundaries are much older than the shire itself, their origins concerned with the ownership and control of Iron Age and Roman Britain.

The Shape of Things

WILTSHIRE IS THE LARGEST inland county in Southern England. Within its boundaries it displays a great variety of landscapes, and it shares many characteristics with its neighbours. Wiltshire's scenery is the result of millennia of human activity, moulding and modifying the land in order to make a living. But it is the land itself - its shape and composition - that has underpinned how such livings might be made. The raw material for life in Wiltshire, therefore, must be understood in terms of its geology.

The solid geology of Wiltshire consists of a series of sedimentary rocks deposited one layer on top of another. The oldest rocks of the series, the limestones of the Cotswolds, are exposed along the county's north-western flank, from Bradford on Avon to Malmesbury and Sherston, and including the famous stone-quarrying region around Corsham and Box. The youngest rocks, the Tertiary sands and clays of the Hampshire Basin, overlie the chalk in parts of Wiltshire's south-east tip, and produce the characteristic wooded heathland of the New Forest edge. An imaginary drive from Southampton across Wiltshire via Devizes to Cirencester, therefore, would entail a journey back through geological time.

Most of such a journey would be spent crossing the high chalklands, between Salisbury and Devizes, and then dropping on to the older claylands around Chippenham. Three large blocks of chalk downland - Cranborne Chase, Salisbury Plain, and the Marlborough Downs - occupy most of southern and eastern Wiltshire, and account for more than half the county's land mass. In places, for example the Savernake area, the chalk has been mantled by a younger deposit of rock, known as Clay-with-Flints, which favours woodland. Dividing the three blocks of chalkland are the Vales of Wardour and Pewsey, which are both the result of the chalk strata having folded and weathered away, exposing the older rocks beneath. In Pewsey Vale and around Devizes Upper Greensand outcrops, producing heavy but fertile soils, and deep holloways where roads cut through, as at Potterne. In Wardour Vale, around Tisbury and Chilmark, older limestones beneath the greensand are revealed, and have been exploited for building stone.

Heading north from Devizes the traveller leaves the greensand and descends into the claylands which extend across much of North Wiltshire, and which have resulted in a relatively flat terrain and heavy, poorly-drained soils. Dividing the two main clay deposits, the Kimmeridge and

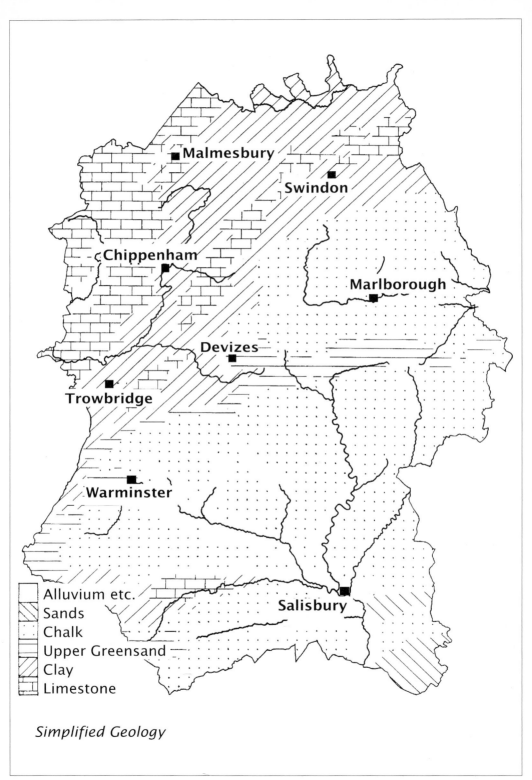

Malmesbury

Swindon

Chippenham

Marlborough

Devizes

Trowbridge

Warminster

Salisbury

Alluvium etc.
Sands
Chalk
Upper Greensand
Clay
Limestone

Simplified Geology

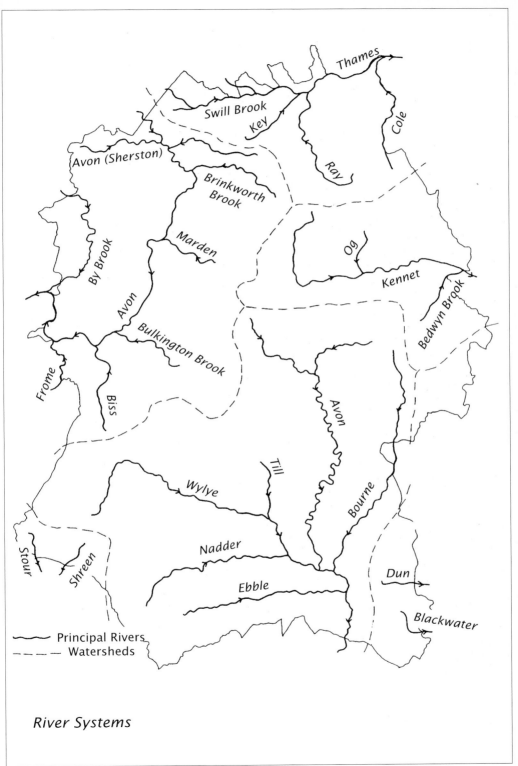

Thames

Swill Brook

Key

Cole

Avon (Sherston)

Ray

Brinkworth Brook

Marden

By Brook

Og

Avon

Kennet

Bedwyn Brook

Bulkington Brook

Frome

Biss

Avon

Bourne

Till

Wylye

Nadder

Stour

Shreen

Ebble

Dun

Blackwater

—— Principal Rivers
- - - - Watersheds

River Systems

Oxford Clays, runs a ridge of harder, very miscellaneous rock, known as the Corallian Beds, which extends from the Steeple Ashton area northeastwards to Lyneham and Wootton Bassett. Crossing this ridge at Derry Hill, the traveller descends once more to the clay around Chippenham, and then gradually the scenery changes to the gentle limestone plateau of the Cotswolds around Malmesbury.

The highest points of Wiltshire, Tan Hill and Milk Hill (295m), are companions along an impressive line of chalk downs overlooking Pewsey Vale. Nearby, above Bishop's Cannings, is the watershed of the three river systems which drain nearly the whole county, and which flow into three different seas. Virtually all South Wiltshire is drained by the Salisbury or Christchurch Avon, and its main tributaries, the Bourne, Wylye, Nadder, and Ebble, which combine near Wilton and Salisbury, and leave the county below Downton. To the north of Tan Hill the rest of the Marlborough Downs is drained by tributaries of the River Thames. The most important is the Kennet, which flows past Avebury to Marlborough, and leaves Wiltshire below Ramsbury. The headwaters of the Thames itself meander for a few miles along the county's northern border, but most of the Wiltshire Cotswolds and claylands are drained by the Bristol Avon or its tributary, the By Brook. The Avon's headwaters rise beyond Malmesbury, where they join to flow south in a great loop through Chippenham and Bradford, leaving the county at Limpley Stoke on their way to Bath and Bristol, and the Severn estuary at Avonmouth.

Wiltshire Working

UNTIL THE ARRIVAL in Wiltshire of engineering and other factory-based industries during the nineteenth century, the majority of the county's workforce was employed either on the land, or in processing one or other of the products of the land, notably wool. And most of those not directly involved in agriculture or clothmaking laboured to provide goods and services for those who were. Farming practices, before artificial fertilizers became available, had to be tailored to exploit the natural resources of the land to best effect, and so varied across the regions of Wiltshire, depending on the type and quality of the soil. Geology and farming were therefore linked.

Throughout the chalklands until Victorian times the classic farming economy was geared to arable production, by using all the different soils and terrains available. Typically this meant growing crops in open fields on the best land, which was generally the chalky loam of the hillslopes and valley sides. Fertility was maintained by running sheep on the rough downland during the day, and folding them on the fields at night, so that their manure enriched the soil. Grass grown in riverside meadows enabled large flocks to be over-wintered. The system was slow to break down, and many communities retained their open fields, with common meadows and downland, until the nineteenth century.

On the claylands, where arable farming was less successful, the predominant activity was dairying, and the main product was cheese. Enclosure of common fields tended to occur much earlier here, during the sixteenth and seventeenth centuries, so that land could be converted to permanent pasture. With the arrival of the railways liquid milk produced for the doorsteps of distant towns became more profitable than cheesemaking, and that industry virtually disappeared. 'Chalk and Cheese' has nevertheless remained a popular expression to describe the geological and farming differences between South and North Wiltshire.

Mixed arable farming in the south and dairying in the north were not, however, the only ways of exploiting the land. Some areas of rich soils thrown up by the greensand or Corallian ridge were suitable for market gardening and fruit growing. Dairying for butter production took place in the south-west corner of Wiltshire, and along the county's eastern and western fringes were large areas of managed woodlands. On parts of the claylands pig-rearing and curing were important, since pigs fed on the

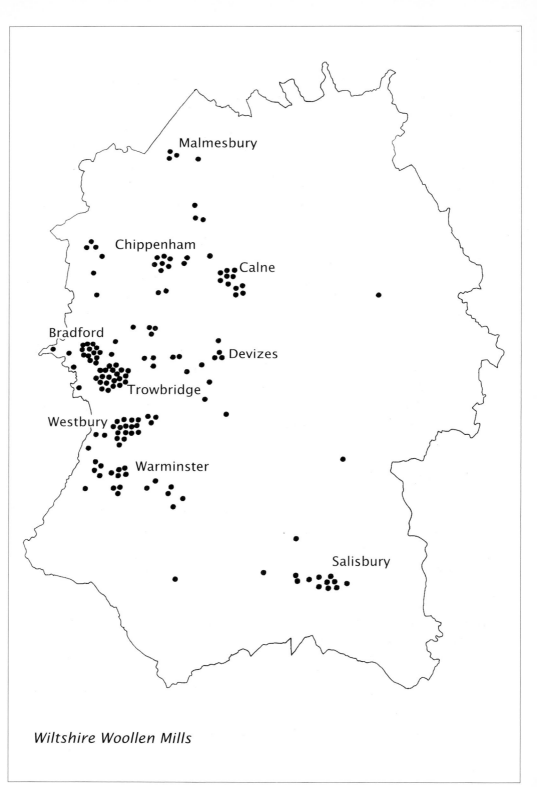

Malmesbury

Chippenham

Calne

Bradford

Devizes

Trowbridge

Westbury

Warminster

Salisbury

Wiltshire Woollen Mills

by-products of cheesemaking.

The most significant by-product of chalkland farming was wool from the downland flocks, and a vigorous clothmaking industry developed first around Salisbury, then by the later middle ages in the Cotswolds, and eventually all over the claylands of the Wiltshire-Somerset border. Apart from the process of fulling, which was carried out in adapted watermills, clothmaking was undertaken as a series of domestic processes, until a factory-based system emerged in the later-eighteenth century. This industry, which came to dominate the life and economy of West Wiltshire, declined in the face of competition from elsewhere during the Victorian period, and some of the factories were converted to other uses, including rubber manufacture or meat products.

Alongside the commonplace have always been the specialist industries, such as quarrying along the Cotswold limestone belt (especially around Bradford, Box and Corsham), as well as at Swindon and in the Vale of Wardour. On the claylands, where building stone was not available, brickworks were established, and iron ore was extracted during the nineteenth century at Westbury and Seend. Malting and brewing became important industries in several Wiltshire towns, alongside various kinds of engineering works, as well as the usual administrative, banking, innkeeping, and commercial services.

A Pattern of People

JUST AS GEOLOGY has affected agriculture, so agriculture has affected the pattern of settlements. As a general rule the chalkland and greensand valleys of South and East Wiltshire display ribbons of compact villages and hamlets, ranged along both sides of their river, and there are relatively few isolated houses away from the main settlement. In the claylands and Cotswolds of North and West Wiltshire, too, compact or nucleated villages may once have predominated, although spread across the countryside in no discernible pattern. But one effect of Tudor and later enclosure for dairying was to sprinkle single farms among their pasture fields away from the villages. In some parts, too, new or enlarged settlements of poor cottages emerged, scattered around surviving portions of common land; in West Wiltshire, many of these communities, such as Southwick and Dilton Marsh, were engaged in the domestic clothmaking industry centred on their nearby towns.

Reliable and comprehensive population statistics do not exist for Wiltshire as a whole before the beginning of the nineteenth century. There were then nearly 200,000 people living in the county, about one-third of the present total (Swindon included). By 1850 most towns and villages had increased their population, and the county total stood just above 250,000. Thereafter the towns, especially Swindon, continued to grow, but most rural parishes began a long and slow decline, as sons and daughters left to seek their fortunes either in London, or the other industrial centres of England, or overseas. The county population did not reach 300,000 until 1930, and the increase from 1850 could be entirely accommodated by the growth of Swindon over the same period.

By examining the results of the 1851 census it is possible to glimpse the settlement pattern of Wiltshire, before emigration, railway travel, industrialization, agricultural depression, and the burgeoning national population all served to distort the traditional picture. Population densities, of course, were highest in the towns, especially Salisbury, Trowbridge and Devizes. Next highest were the towns and countryside of the clothmaking and quarrying regions of West Wiltshire, from Warminster northwards to Chippenham. Elsewhere on the claylands and Cotswolds the density was lower but fairly uniform, but as the eye moves south-eastward across the map of Wiltshire the population appears to thin out, and is lowest of all in the chalkland areas around Amesbury and Netheravon, and east of Salisbury. Paradoxically, the thinly populated chalkland was the area where most people lived in close proximity to each other in compact villages, but separated by large tracts of empty downs; whereas in parts of the more densely settled claylands there were fewer close neighbours, because farms and cottages were spread more evenly across the countryside.

Matters of settlement and population are important for this study because people's local circumstances colour their outlook. A cottager in a Wylye valley village, hemmed in by an adjacent manor house or barn belonging to his landlord and ultimate employer, the squire, may form political and religious views, and see his own place in the local community, rather differently from a smallholder or cottage weaver a few miles away, on the outskirts of Westbury, who claimed the freehold of his dwelling, had no immediate neighbours, and was beholden to nobody.

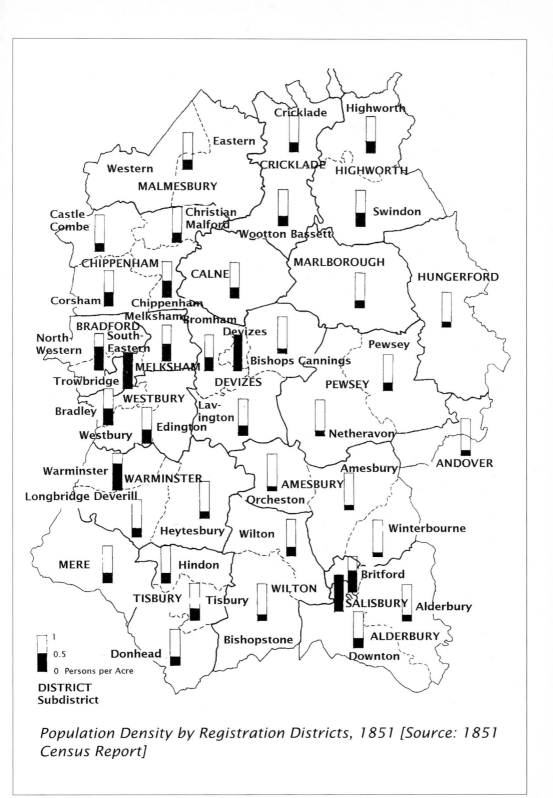

Population Density by Registration Districts, 1851 [Source: 1851 Census Report]

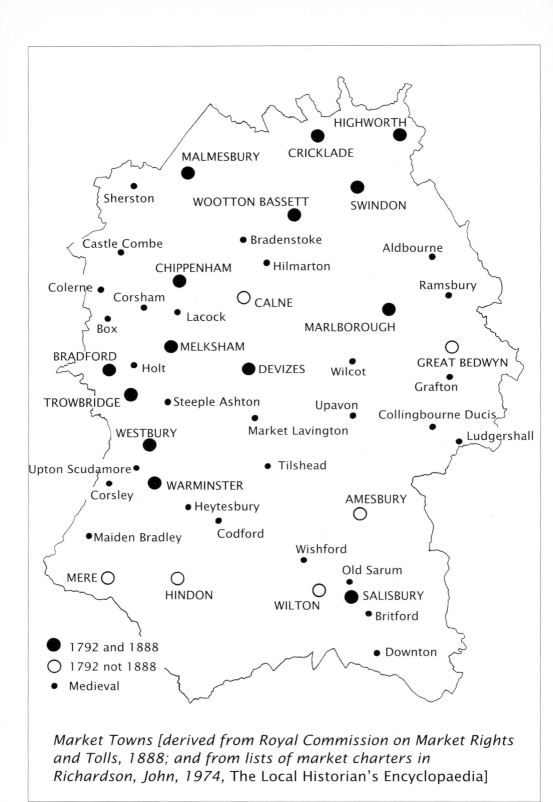

Market Towns [derived from Royal Commission on Market Rights and Tolls, 1888; and from lists of market charters in Richardson, John, 1974, The Local Historian's Encyclopaedia]

Although most Wiltshire men and women until the nineteenth century lived in villages or the countryside, towns have been a feature of Wiltshire life since Saxon times; indeed there were Roman towns, as we have seen, before Wiltshire as an entity existed. Our present pattern of towns evolved over a long period, from the seventh or eighth century to the thirteenth. Malmesbury, Bradford, Calne, Chippenham and Wilton are among the oldest Saxon foundations, with Marlborough, Old Sarum, and Cricklade perhaps arriving later in the Saxon period. For two centuries after the Norman conquest several hundred new towns were established in England and Wales, as the population rose, and they include Devizes, Salisbury, and Hindon in Wiltshire. Many existing villages were converted to small towns (not always successfully), or attempted to take on some of the functions of a town, for example by holding a weekly market. Urbanization of this kind occurred particularly during the thirteenth century, and had come to an end by 1300. The only new town in Wiltshire thereafter was the railway town of New Swindon, after 1840. Of nearly fifty Wiltshire places which at some time had urban aspirations, only twenty still figured among a list of market towns in 1792, and by 1888 only fourteen held markets.

Of Wiltshire's towns only Salisbury in the middle ages (which became the focus of an extensive diocese and the regional capital of central Southern England), and Swindon in recent times, have ever had more than local significance. For the most part they have lived in symbiosis with their surrounding countryside, depending on its produce and producers for their livelihood, and in return providing specialist services and commodities, and opportunities for trade and exchange, which villages were too small to organize for themselves. In this capacity towns have played a crucial part in shaping the community areas with which this study is concerned, and their individual roles are considered later.

Academic Circles

OUR MEANDERING through historical geography has led us so far to consider such diverse matters as: the tenacity of boundaries, the problems of governing a Saxon kingdom, Roman estates, the relationship between geology and agriculture, clothmaking, settlement patterns, and the function of towns. Once explored and expressed, the links between landscapes, processes, and communities are quite obvious. And they seem to offer at least a partial explanation of how Wiltshire, as a series of interlocking communities, functions now, based on how it has functioned in the past. In the sections which follow we shall present some of the historical evidence for the existence of Wiltshire as a community, and for the identity of smaller community areas within it. This evidence, based on social, administrative, and economic considerations, can be superimposed on what we have discovered so far about the nature and variety of our county.

In taking this course, and embarking on what might be called the 'chalk-and-cheese' debate, it must be confessed that we are not trailblazing, but merely following a long tradition. Thomas Fuller, writing of Wiltshire before 1661, has given us perhaps the first and most eloquent summary of the matter: 'I have heard a wise man say that an ox left to himself would, of all England, choose to live in the north, a sheep in the south part hereof, and a man in the middle betwixt both, as partaking of the pleasure of the plain, and the wealth of the deep country.'

Nor is the measurement of Wiltshire's differences anything new. It can be traced back to John Aubrey, who died in 1697, and who, wishing to determine the proportion of downland to vale, used a pair of scissors to cut up a map into the respective parts, which he then weighed. The first map specifically drawn to depict the land use of Wiltshire was compiled in 1794, by Thomas Davis of Longleat, in the course of a report on the county's agriculture. During the 1930s a Land Utilization Survey was undertaken, which reported on Wiltshire in 1940.

At national and international level the study of towns and other significant settlements as 'central places' began on the continent during the nineteenth century, and was renewed in Germany and Britain from the 1930s and 1940s onwards. Among the English pioneers in this field was H.E. Bracey, who published in 1952 a book based on his research into social provision in Wiltshire. His painstaking work, invaluable for the present study, included sending out questionnaires and analyzing all kinds of social data, which enabled him to draw a series of central place maps of the county. Later, during the quantitative revolution in human geography during the 1960s, such research techniques were refined and improved.

Meanwhile the development across disciplines of the study of landscape history, the wider availability of historical sources in libraries and record offices, and the advancement of local history as an academic subject, have all opened new vistas on an old debate. One of the most relevant to the present study has been the recognition of distinctive countrysides, which are united not only by topography and agriculture, but also by economic and social concerns. To such regions the French word *pays* has been applied, and the idea, first formulated during the 1950s, has been elaborated by landscape historians in recent years and is now widely accepted.

Moonraker Pride

BECAUSE THE SHIRE was a unit of medieval government, overseen by the sheriff, its identity was maintained through the middle ages. Indeed among the leading families, who were called upon from the late-thirteenth century to assist the sheriff as justices of the peace, a corporate loyalty developed towards their shire. And this sense of county identity was so strong by the time of the civil war that one historian (Alan Everitt) has suggested that, 'the England of 1640 resembled a union of partially-independent county-states or communities, each with its own distinct ethos and loyalty'. Elizabethan reforms during the sixteenth century had in fact strengthened county solidarity at gentry level, by placing ever more administrative responsibilities on the magistrates, who were summoned to meet every three months. These Quarter Sessions, as they became known, between the sixteenth and nineteenth centuries evolved, in fact, as a nascent county council, employing staff, controlling certain functions (such as prisons, bridge maintenance, and weights and measures), and supervising the parochial responsibilities of road repair and poor relief.

In other respects medieval and early modern Wiltshire was by no means an 'independent county-state'. Several of the county's largest landowners, such as the Bishop of Winchester and the Abbot of Glastonbury, were based outside Wiltshire and controlled domains extending across county boundaries. The wealthy merchants of Salisbury had their trading links with Southampton, and the interests of the West Wiltshire clothiers straddled the Somerset border. Some of the social differences which we have begun to detect within Wiltshire existed in fact across a much larger area. Most dialect speakers in the county, for instance, except in the north-east, pronounced initial f as v, and s as z, a peculiarity which they shared with other south-western counties from Gloucestershire and Hampshire westwards, but not with their fellow Wiltshiremen around Swindon and the Thames Valley. Likewise, support for the royalist cause during the civil war was strong in the Wiltshire chalklands, but also in Blackmore Vale and beyond, across the Somerset and Dorset borders; in West Wiltshire and East Somerset, by contrast, the clothmaking population leant towards Parliament and Puritanism.

This particular 'chalk and cheese' distinction was noticed by Aubrey, who along with other unsavoury characteristics (melancholy, plump, malicious), reported that North Wiltshire inhabitants were, 'more apt to be fanatiques'; South Wiltshiremen, by contrast, were hardworking, and too busy, 'to read and contemplate of religion'. As a 'church and chapel' divide (church = chalk, chapel = cheese), this difference persisted, and was eloquently recorded two centuries later, by the 1851 religious census. It may be explained, in part at least, by the effect of the 'closed' villages of the chalklands, controlled by resident, Anglican, squires, compared with the more open, free-thinking, society of smallholders and clothworkers on the clay.

Despite the turmoil of the civil war, it was during the sixteenth and seventeenth centuries that a recognisable county gentry emerged, in Wiltshire as elsewhere, and began to display an interest in the genealogical intertwinings which bound their families together, and a patriotism which prompted them to contemplate writing a county history. Such a proposal was discussed, according to John Aubrey, in 1659, significantly, 'at a meeting of gentlemen at the Devises for choosing of knights for the shire'. Nothing came of it (apart from Aubrey's own historical collections), but the spirit and the impetus were clearly present.

In another respect, however, Wiltshire had perhaps led the field in county loyalty. The first reference to a Wiltshire Feast held annually in London by gentlemen of the county (to raise money for apprenticing

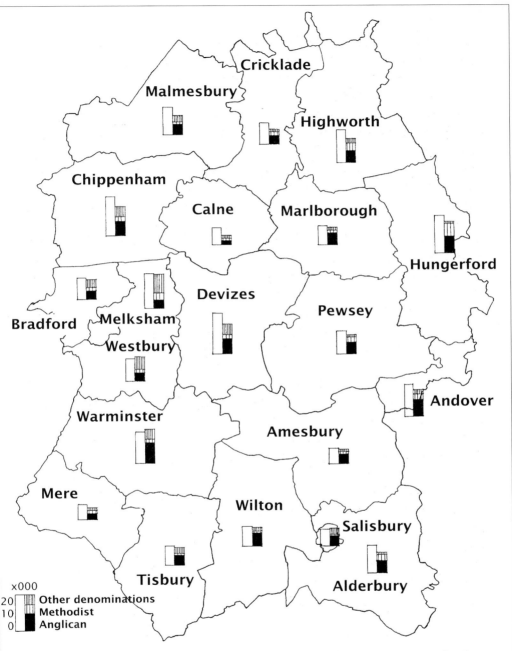

Cricklade
Malmesbury
Highworth
Chippenham
Calne
Marlborough
Hungerford
Bradford
Melksham
Devizes
Pewsey
Westbury
Andover
Warminster
Amesbury
Mere
Wilton
Salisbury
Tisbury
Alderbury

x000
20 — Other denominations
10 — Methodist
0 — Anglican

Religious Census, 1851, showing attendance at Anglican, Methodist, and other nonconformist places of worship, compared with the total population. The census is flawed, in that worshippers attending two or more services were counted each time, so that it is impossible to deduce the total numbers of worshippers and abstainers.

Wiltshire natives, or other charities) occurs in 1654, and the preacher whose sermon preceded the feast praised the organizers, 'who had the honour to give the nation a precedent'. The feast led to similar gatherings elsewhere, and perhaps ultimately (in 1817) to the foundation of a Society of Wiltshiremen in London, which, as the Wiltshire Society, still exists.

During the eighteenth and nineteenth centuries a plethora of organizations emerged which had 'Wiltshire' in their title, and thus stimulated the county's sense of identity. Among the most important were probably the Wiltshire Regiment, so designated in 1782 in order to promote recruiting locally, and the Wiltshire Archaeological and Natural History Society in 1853, which encouraged the study of various aspects of the county.

The sobriquet 'moonrakers' for Wiltshire inhabitants was in use by 1819 and, as a derogatory tale against Wiltshiremen, so stupid as to try to rake the moon out of a pond believing it to be a cheese, the moonraking story existed before 1785, and perhaps before 1765. At first, and perhaps through most of the nineteenth century, the expression seems to have been intended as an insult, rather like the couplet which is occasionally still heard, 'Wiltshire born and Wiltshire bred, Strong in the arm and thick in the head.' It may be significant that the Wiltshire Regiment in 1782 adopted the nickname 'Springers', not 'Moonrakers'. By the 1850s the now familiar twist in the tale was current, whereby the Wiltshiremen were actually raking brandy kegs from the pond, and outwitted a passing excisemen with their feigned stupidity. This became the 'authorized version' when Edward Slow's dialect poem, 'The Wiltshire Moonrakers', was published in 1881. The connection with smuggling (which was quite plausible, since contraband regularly crossed Wiltshire by night until the nineteenth century) may have suggested itself through the word 'moonshine', which was in use for smuggled goods by 1785. Excise was introduced in 1643, so in its developed form the story cannot possibly be older than the seventeenth century.

The Old Regime

FOR SOME ADMINISTRATIVE FUNCTIONS the county has always been too large and unwieldy, and so smaller units have been adopted by both church and state. We have already explored the shadowy origins of one of these, the grouping of tithings known as the hundred. Throughout the middle ages and until the reforms of the 1830s (and to a lesser extent even later) hundreds functioned as the main secular administrative and judicial unit between the parish and the shire. Even when they lost their significance, the later boundaries were drawn against the background of their centuries' old existence. Great medieval magnates, such as the Bishop of Winchester, complicated the original arrangement by withdrawing parishes from one hundred and placing them in another, sometimes geographically remote. Thus Wroughton (near Swindon), Ham (near Hungerford), and Westwood (near Bradford) were all transferred to the bishop's hundred of Elstub and Everley, with its nucleus on Salisbury Plain. During the middle ages, too, several of the smaller hundreds were amalgamated. Hundreds are generally named from their original meeting-place, or moot. This may be a village or small town, such as Melksham, Amesbury, Chippenham, or Alderbury; or it may be from some natural or manmade landmark in the countryside, such as Swanborough (a barrow in Pewsey Vale), Kinwardstone (a standing stone near Burbage), Whorwellsdown, or Cawdon (hills near Steeple Ashton and Wilton respectively). Hundredal centres, therefore, offer some of the earliest evidence for 'central places' in Wiltshire.

The ecclesiastical equivalent of the secular hundred was the rural deanery, which stood between the parish and the archdeaconry or diocese as an intermediate level of church government and discipline from the middle ages onward, and like the hundred may have been based on more ancient antecedents. Wiltshire's nine medieval deaneries suggest a very early partition of the county based on significant ecclesiastical foci, such as Avebury, Malmesbury, and Potterne. This arrangement perhaps predates the emergence of Wilton as shire capital, since its small and awkward deanery appears to have been an afterthought carved from one or more of its neighbours. In 1872 seven of the Wiltshire deaneries were subdivided.

The basic unit of church government since the tenth century has been the parish. This evolved from earlier, larger territories created by the

Chippenham

Malmesbury

Highworth, Cricklade and Staple

North Damerham

Kingsbridge

Chippenham

Calne

Selkley

Ramsbury

Bradford

Melksham

Potterne and Cannings

Kinwardstone

Whorwellsdown

Swanborough

Westbury

Elstub and Everleigh

Warminster

Heytesbury

Amesbury

Branch and Dole

Underditch

Mere

Cawden

Alderbury

Dunworth

and

Cadworth

Frustfield

Parishes detached from their Hundreds

Chalke

Downton

Principal Hundred Divisions, 1831

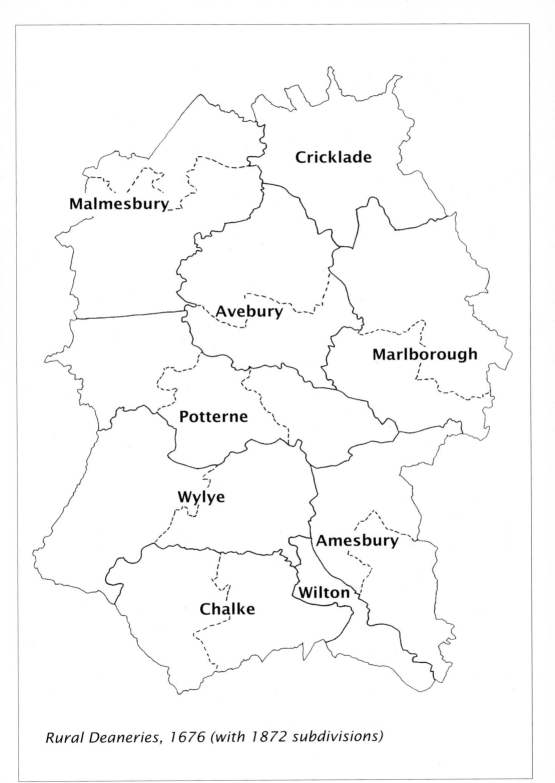

Cricklade

Malmesbury

Avebury

Marlborough

Potterne

Wylye

Amesbury

Wilton

Chalke

Rural Deaneries, 1676 (with 1872 subdivisions)

evangelizing activities of the early Christian missionaries, who centred their work on churches known as minsters. The minsters, which were often established at hundredal centres (for example, Warminster) acted as headquarters for communities of priests, who preached and established satellite churches (sometimes known as 'field-churches') in the surrounding countryside. Tithe payments to pay for priests were inaugurated during the tenth century, and thereafter many of the field-churches became independent of their minsters, and established a parish around them (often, as we have seen, based on existing tithing boundaries) from which they received tithe payments. The relationship between minster and field-church (regarded at first as that between mother and daughter) was thereby broken in most cases, although some of the daughter churches did not achieve their own parishes. Thus at Westbury until the nineteenth century the old territory based on a minster church in Westbury itself became the parish, and Westbury's daughters, at Bratton, Dilton, and Heywood, were merely chapels-of-ease.

As well as its role as the unit of corporate religious worship, the parish figured from the sixteenth century also as a local government body, known as the parish vestry, responsible in particular for road maintenance and poor relief within its own boundaries. The Victorians began to see these religious and secular aspects of parish life separately, and distinguished between civil and ecclesiastical parishes, often redrawing their boundaries along different lines. Some sparsely populated areas, such as parts of Savernake Forest, had never been regarded as lying within any parish, and were known as extra-parochial places. They became civil parishes, or were included in the boundaries of their neighbours. In 1894, as part of local government reforms, elected civil parish councils were created, with a range of purely local responsibilities. During the later twentieth century many ecclesiastical parishes have been amalgamated, or have been grouped into 'team ministries'. Historians refer, therefore, to ancient parishes, civil parishes, ecclesiastical parishes, and extra-parochial places, all with different shades of meaning.

The Victorian Innovators

BEGINNING with the Poor Law Act of 1834 (just before Victoria's accession), and culminating in the creation of urban and rural districts in 1894, the Victorians set about creating and re-creating tiers of local government to administer an ever-increasing range of services. The boundaries of the various new authorities borrowed from their predecessors, but seldom coincided exactly.

The division of the country into poor law unions after 1834 aimed to improve the efficiency of poor relief by transferring responsibility from parish vestries working individually to groups, or 'unions', of parishes, each administering a workhouse. In Wiltshire much of the structure of poor law unions was determined by one man, Charles A'Court, in the course of two months during 1835. His task, unlike later local government changes, was not to fragment a large entity (the county) into smaller units; rather it was an exercise in combining small units (parishes) into larger entities. He was not, therefore, constrained by the county boundary, and indeed 11 of the 26 unions to which Wiltshire parishes belonged lay in more than one county. The poor law reformers, in fact, envisaged that in course of time the union would supplant the county as the basic unit of local government (the 'unitary authority' in modern parlance), and that the county would fade into insignificance.

The principal determining factor for drawing union boundaries was claimed to have been the suitability of local people to administer them. Apart from those derived from local knowledge and intuition, therefore, they did not necessarily reflect existing loyalties, hinterlands, or territories (although clearly the old hundredal boundaries were considered). Neither were they the product of widespread prior consultation and debate, and they presented wide discrepancies in area, population, and numbers of parishes united. Once established, however, they tended to create or reinforce territories based on the towns and union workhouses from which they were administered.

Almost immediately, with the introduction of civil registration of births, marriages, and deaths in 1837, the union boundaries were adopted for the new registration districts, Later legislation, in 1872, used the union (from which urban areas had been removed) as the basis for the new rural sanitary districts, the forerunners of rural district councils. The unions thus provided significant pieces of the local government jigsaw

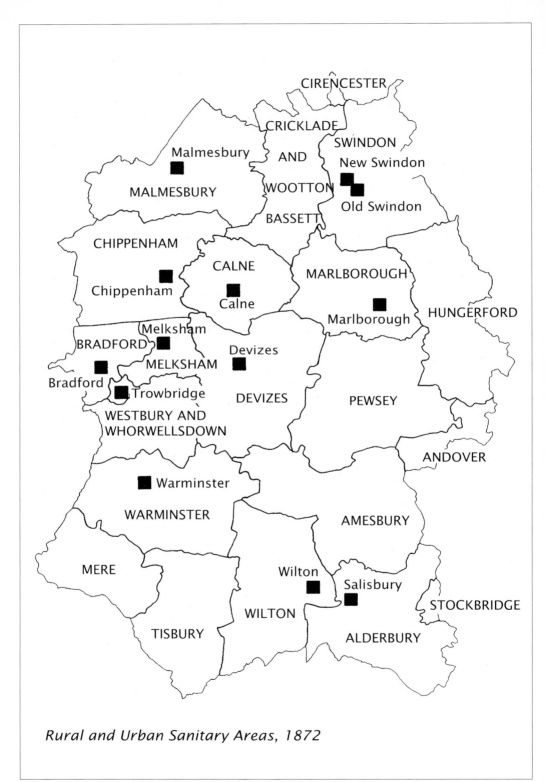

Rural and Urban Sanitary Areas, 1872

CRICK-
LADE

MALMESBURY

SWINDON

CHIPPENHAM

CALNE

MARLBOROUGH

TROWBRIDGE

DEVIZES

EVERLEIGH AND
PEWSEY

WARMINSTER

AMESBURY

HINDON

SALISBURY

Highway Districts, 1864

which the Victorians completed in 1894.

The problem with using unions in this way was their awkward disregard for county boundaries, which meant that whenever service provision was to be funded and organized on a county basis, another system of division had to be found. As railways proliferated across the Victorian countryside, the apparently obsolescent main road system, which was administered by turnpike trusts, fell on hard times. Legislation of 1862 passed responsibility for roads, as each turnpike act expired, to the county magistrates, and highway districts were established to supervise them. And since many union boundaries were unsuitable, the county used another, older, system of internal division, the petty sessions districts.

Petty sessions – meetings of a group of local magistrates from a specific area for a particular purpose – evolved in Wiltshire gradually from the sixteenth century. At first the geographical scope of these groupings may have been influenced by a tendency during this period to partition the county into six divisions or combinations of hundreds, based on Salisbury, Warminster, Marlborough, Devizes, Chippenham and Westbury or Trowbridge. But during the eighteenth century we find the magistrates of a single hundred (or two neighbouring hundreds) meeting in petty sessions, and at the same time there was also growing up a tendency to regard the four quarterly meetings of magistrates from the whole county (the Quarter Sessions), held at Salisbury, Warminster, Marlborough and Devizes, as relevant only to south, west, east and north Wiltshire respectively. This fourfold division had apparently replaced the earlier sixfold division, so that at the beginning of the nineteenth century, it has been suggested, Wiltshire was in many ways more like four counties than one.

In fact the semi-official subdivision of the county into various larger and smaller areas for the purposes of local government and justice was well established by this period. Under the burden of Victorian legislation petty sessions became better organized into mappable districts, and so these formed the basis of the highway districts. Their boundaries were not, however, identical. Trowbridge highway district was an amalgamation of five small petty sessions divisions (Bradford, Melksham, Trowbridge, Westbury, Whorwellsdown), and Salisbury petty sessions division was divided into Salisbury and Amesbury highway districts.

By the 1870s, therefore, two systems of administrative boundaries had evolved, the one based on dividing the county into districts, the other in amalgamating parishes into unions. County government, which included the employment of paid officials, such as a county surveyor, the constabulary, and the staff of the county gaols and lunatic asylum, was vested in the magistrates meeting in Quarter Sessions, but this authority had little contact with the bodies operating within the structure of the poor law unions. A Highways Act in 1878 was the first to forge a link between the two, by giving rural sanitary districts highways responsibilities. In consequence Quarter Sessions established a Boundary Committee, and between 1878 and 1894 various measures were taken to marry the two systems. These involved principally the transferring of Wiltshire parishes from out-county unions into Wiltshire unions, uniting or altering divided parishes, and in some cases altering the county boundary to accord with union boundaries.

The new structure of elected county, district, and parish administration, introduced under legislation of 1888 and 1894, established urban and rural district councils based on the 1872 sanitary districts. It remained largely intact until 1929, when the old poor law unions were abolished, and in consequence the county was required by legislation to review all its boundaries and recommend changes. As a result, in 1934 nearly fifty parishes were abolished, and twelve small rural districts were merged into six.

This pre-war administrative structure survived for forty years, until the 1974 local government reorganization created five districts out of the thirteen urban and twelve rural authorities. Their boundaries followed those of the rural districts, as follows- Kennet (Devizes, Pewsey, Marlborough and Ramsbury); North Wiltshire (Calne and Chippenham, Cricklade and Wootton Bassett, Malmesbury); Salisbury (Amesbury, Mere and Tisbury, Salisbury and Wilton); Thamesdown (Highworth); West Wiltshire (Bradford and Melksham, Warminster and Westbury). A further wide-ranging review conducted twenty years later determined to retain in Wiltshire a two-tier structure of local government, based on the county (less Thamesdown) and the other four existing districts. Thamesdown became a unitary authority, renamed Swindon Borough, in April 1997, and apart from certain joint and agency arrangements, is now administered entirely separately from the rest of the historic county.

For over a century county, district, and parish government has been by elected councillors, and it is to the democratic process that we owe

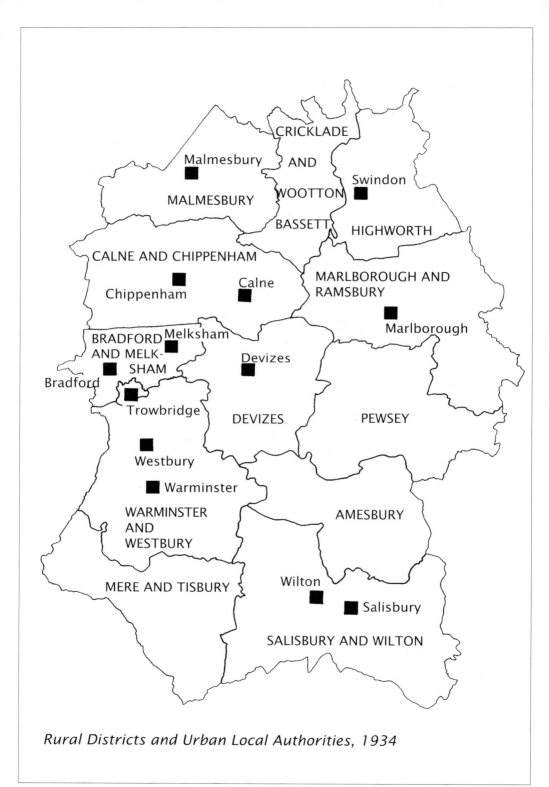

CRICKLADE
AND
WOOTTON
BASSETT

Malmesbury

MALMESBURY

Swindon

HIGHWORTH

CALNE AND CHIPPENHAM

Chippenham

Calne

MARLBOROUGH AND
RAMSBURY

Marlborough

BRADFORD
AND MELK-
SHAM

Melksham

Devizes

Bradford

Trowbridge

DEVIZES

PEWSEY

Westbury

Warminster

WARMINSTER
AND
WESTBURY

AMESBURY

MERE AND TISBURY

Wilton

Salisbury

SALISBURY AND WILTON

Rural Districts and Urban Local Authorities, 1934

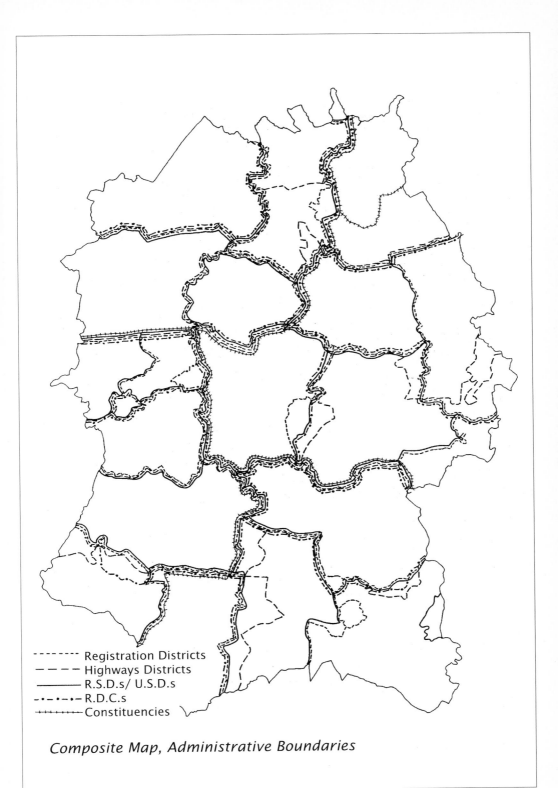

Registration Districts
Highways Districts
R.S.D.s/ U.S.D.s
R.D.C.s
Constituencies

Composite Map, Administrative Boundaries

one further tradition of dividing Wiltshire, the Parliamentary constituencies. The electorate of Wiltshire before Parliamentary reform in 1832 was restricted to a very small and unrepresentative elite minority. About 1,200 electors (less than 1% of Wiltshire's adult population) returned 34 members to Parliament in 1831, and we have already examined the growing importance of this landowning and political elite in creating the idea of a Wiltshire 'community' since medieval times.

The pre-reform representation was based on boroughs, with two county seats, and it was not until 1885, with the franchise greatly increased, that Wiltshire was divided geographically into a number of constituencies. This rearrangement created five divisions, based on Chippenham, Cricklade, Devizes, Westbury and Wilton, with a sixth member returned by Salisbury as a Parliamentary borough. The constituency names seem to have been selected from the pre-reform tradition of Parliamentary boroughs rather than from considerations of contemporary population or county government, so that Swindon lay within the Cricklade division, and Trowbridge within the Westbury division. The division boundaries were modified in 1918 by the abolition of Salisbury's borough seat, the creation of a Swindon division, and the redrawing of the Chippenham, Devizes and Westbury divisions, in order to bring them into line with local government areas. Subsequent population changes have dictated further alterations, including a second constituency for Swindon.

Despite the apparent complexities which our Victorian ancestors wove into their systems of administrative boundaries, when those boundaries are superimposed the overall impression is one of continuity. Many boundaries were in fact shared by the poor law unions, the sanitary, highway and rural districts, and the constituencies. Only along Wiltshire's eastern and south-western fringes, and around Salisbury and Trowbridge, have there been significant discrepancies.

Town and Country

THE PARTITIONING of Wiltshire for administrative convenience, however repeatedly and consistently done, has not necessarily reflected the local areas to which ordinary people have felt that they belong, and to which they have owed their allegiance. Those feelings depend as much on patterns of work and travel, shopping and schooling, entertainment and leisure. Sensitive and appropriate local government, which is the aim of the community areas approach, will always try to coincide with such patterns, and local authority boundaries, once established, may serve to enhance or modify them. Thus school catchment areas, even if arbitrarily drawn, tend to dictate the geographical area across which friendships made at school, and continued into later life, are spread.

But it is important also to recognize that county-based government can never be made to coincide precisely with communities based on social and economic identity, the so-called *pays* of the landscape historian, because such communities do not respect county boundaries. Many Wiltshire residents, for example, rely for certain services, and for their employment, on towns such as Bath, Cirencester, Andover, or Shaftesbury, and therefore develop an affinity with communities centred on places outside the county.

Before the nineteenth century it is not easy to find historical sources which enable the boundaries of community life to be mapped across Wiltshire. But the proliferation of information about Wiltshire during the Victorian period can be used to suggest patterns of allegiance and identity. For the twentieth century the data collected by H.E. Bracey during the 1940s are invaluable. We shall examine a variety of evidence, and compare it with the administrative boundaries already described.

One of the best indicators of the extent of a town's hinterland is provided by the lists of village carriers printed in nineteenth-century directories. Carriers had existed since the sixteenth century, and probably earlier, but during the Victorian period they proliferated, so that almost every village had its own carrier, who took produce, parcels and passengers to and from a nearby town once each week or more frequently, generally coinciding with market days. If a village was roughly equidistant from two towns, as occurred in the Vale of Pewsey, the carrier would travel to both, on different days. A few places, such as the upper Avon valley around Enford, had services to three towns, and Mere had

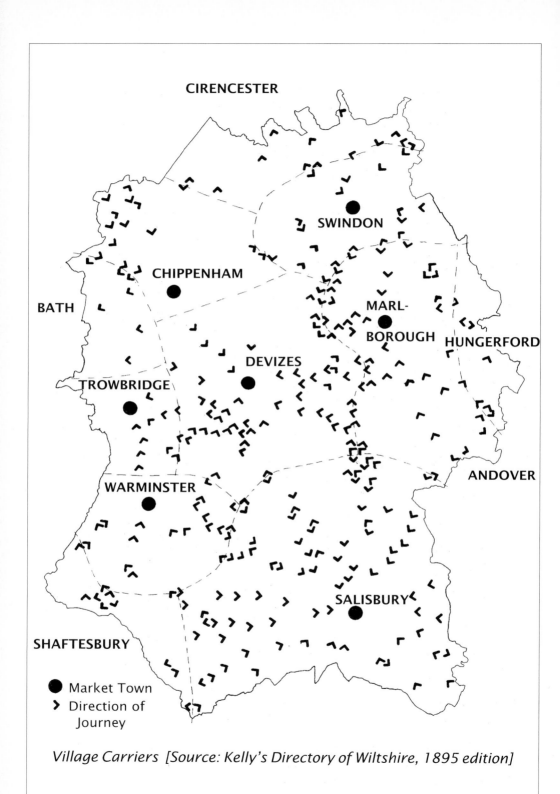

Village Carriers [Source: Kelly's Directory of Wiltshire, 1895 edition]

Railways, Canals, and Stagecoaches [Sources: maps in Victoria County History of Wiltshire, vol.4; and Chandler, John, 1980, Stagecoach operation through Wiltshire]

carriers to Frome, Warminster, Shaftesbury, Gillingham and Wincanton. From the activities of carriers it is possible to gauge shopping patterns and commercial links between towns and villages, and so to map the limits of a particular centre's influence on its surrounding countryside.

On the map of local carriers in 1895 there is a noticeable gap on the Wiltshire claylands. This may in part be the result of a different settlement pattern and agricultural regime, but it is probably influenced largely by the facilities for railway travel in this area. This introduces one of the dynamics for change in community areas, the substitution of a new and more efficient means of travelling between one place and another. The arrival of canal and railway networks across Wiltshire during the nineteenth century led to the demise of the stagecoach and a wholesale redrawing of the communications map. This was to the detriment of some towns, such as Marlborough, Calne, Amesbury and Mere, and the advantage of others, including Swindon, Chippenham and Westbury.

Although the burgeoning of local government responsibilities during the nineteenth and twentieth centuries is not of direct importance to our theme, the command structure devised by county departments to administer their work may be relevant to territorial boundaries. The organization of the Wiltshire constabulary, for example, into police divisions, subdivisions and village police stations, can be reconstructed as they were in 1895, according to information in the trade directory. When plotted on a map this command structure may be compared with the journeys of local carriers at the same date; apart from two police divisions centred on places (Tisbury and Malmesbury) which were not important carriers' destinations, the data show that policemen and carriers were in broad agreement about the extent of the community areas which then existed around local towns.

Many of these towns, especially during the period from about 1870 to 1950, had a stationer, printer or newspaper proprietor who produced annually a trade and local information directory. In some cases this included a section entitled 'village directory', listing principal inhabitants in surrounding villages. Taken together, the principal Wiltshire local directories interlock and overlap to cover most of the county. Weekly local newspapers of the period sampled (the 1890s) had a rather wider coverage, and often expected their readers to be interested in events occurring in places quite remote from their main circulation area. But they generally also had a section each week devoted to 'local intelligence',

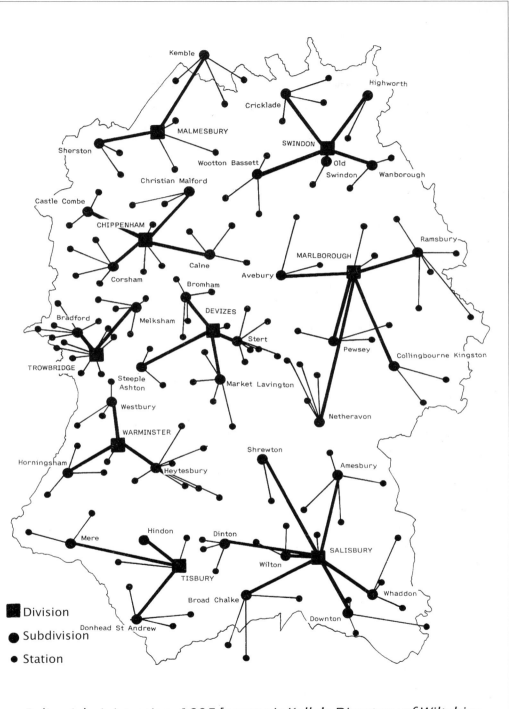

Division

Subdivision

Station

Police Administration, 1895 [source is Kelly's Directory of Wiltshire, 1895 edition]

Shopping Areas, 1950 [Source: Bracey, 1952]

or short reports submitted by amateur correspondents in the villages and towns which they served. These too may be plotted to suggest the sphere of influence of their place of publication.

As we move into the twentieth century, the task of mapping community area boundaries is simplified by the work of H.E. Bracey, mentioned earlier. His research, conducted during the 1940s, included analysis of more than 200 village questionnaires, as well as membership lists, timetables, employees, and many other social data, and so enabled him to draw a series of central place maps of Wiltshire which anticipated by more than a decade the general interest by geographers in the subject. A good example, derived from his questionnaires, plots the 'regular shopping expeditions', or 'weekly or fortnightly visit to town'. It is a fairly crude indicator, since more recent geographers would insist on a hierarchy of shopping towns, depending on the type of product sought. It does however allow a useful comparison with the pattern of carriers' routes fifty years earlier, and could also be compared with Wiltshire structure plan data collected in the 1970s.

The importance of agriculture in the life of the county suggested to Bracey that some indication of farmers' social organization would be important, since it might reflect attendance at markets, and similarities of farming regimes. He therefore obtained details of National Farmers' Union local branches, and discovered that, while much of Wiltshire falls into three large branches, centred on Swindon, Devizes and Salisbury, several of the smaller towns whose marketing role had dwindled, such as Sherston, Melksham, Mere and Calne, nevertheless retained their own N.F.U. branches.

Bracey also attempted more complex, composite plans. He plotted boundaries around each service centre of various organizations and facilities - the British Legion; Women's Institute; Girl Guides; Hospitals; National Farmers' Union; local newspapers; banks; shopping; and grammar schools. He then drew a 'line of best fit' around each service centre, leaving an equal number of individual boundaries on each side, and thus defined 'median areas'. Another useful map included in Bracey's book depicted the catchment areas for secondary modern schools as envisaged under the County Development Plan, 1946. These were an imposed administrative division, but appear to have been determined with accessibility in mind. They are interesting, too, because they depict minor centres as well as the larger shopping towns and service providers.

Secondary Modern School Catchment Areas, 1946 [Source: Bracey, 1952]

Malmesbury

Swindon ⊕

Chippenham ⊕

Calne ⊕

Marlborough ⊕

Melksham ⊕

Bradford ⊕

Devizes ⊕

Trowbridge ⊕

Westbury ⊕

Warminster ⊕

Mere ⊕

Salisbury ⊕

- - - - Police Divisions
———— Shopping Areas
+++++ Median Areas
-×-×-× Carriers

Composite Map, Spheres of Influence

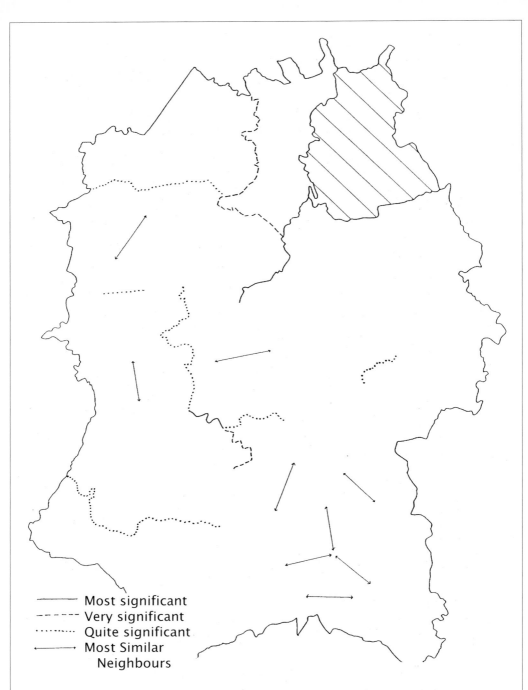

Most Significant Boundaries. This map is derived from a complex scoring system used in the 1993 report (pp.65-8) to assess the significance of the community boundaries as then proposed. Some boundary changes have occurred subsequently.

If we compare the results of Bracey's research with the evidence drawn from earlier periods a coherent picture emerges. As might be expected the hinterlands around Salisbury, Devizes and Swindon are reasonably consistent, and Marlborough, Chippenham and Warminster also have fairly discrete territories. But the positions of all the other west Wiltshire towns are far more precarious and ambiguous, reflecting no doubt the pull of Bath as an over-riding central place beyond the county boundary.

Thus in attempting to determine relevant community area boundaries for the twenty-first century in the light of historical precedents, we can draw on a range of evidence which by and large presents a coherent and consistent picture of the evolution of community allegiance, central places and geographical *pays*. In view of what we have discovered about the tenacity of old boundaries, this is a reassuring conclusion, which seems to justify our historical approach. By using the detailed maps scattered through this chapter we can begin, not only to determine Wiltshire's community areas, but also to describe them individually. This will be the task of Chapter 3. But we still have one piece of unfinished business.

The Swindon Phenomenon

At the 1831 census Swindon was one of five communities in North-East Wiltshire which returned a population of between 1,500 and 2,000; the others were Wootton Bassett, Purton, Cricklade, and Wroughton. Highworth was considerably larger (over 3,000), but the nearest important towns were Cirencester and Marlborough. Each place had its own specialities and idiosyncrasies - Swindon's was quarrying - but all were large Wiltshire parishes with extensive agricultural interests, and broadly similar in outlook.

During the fifty years before 1840 North-East Wiltshire, previously a rather remote district, had been made more accessible to commercial traffic through the opening of canals across it. Swindon, in particular, which had a wharf on the Wilts and Berks Canal, showed signs during the 1820s and 1830s of self-improvement and growing affluence, still apparent in the architecture of Swindon Museum (Apsley House) and its neighbours along Bath Road, Old Town.

In 1836 the Great Western Railway decided that the flat clayland below what is now Old Swindon should be the junction between its line from

London to Bristol, and its spur to Gloucester and Cheltenham. Speculators correctly and immediately predicted that this would result in not only a railway station, but also a depot for housing locomotives. In 1840 it was proposed that the depot should also include a facility to repair and maintain the rolling stock, and (from 1846) to manufacture locomotives. The consequence of these decisions was to enhance the existing settlement (thenceforth Old Swindon) and create an entirely new town (New Swindon). The two retained their separate identities until 1900, but during the 1880s and 1890s houses and streets coalesced on the hillside between them and they became fused together. Between 1851 and 1901 Old and New Swindon together increased their population from 4,879 to 45,006, representing an increase of 822%, ten times the average for England and Wales. Excluding Swindon, Wiltshire's population fell during this period by 8%.

Local government in Victorian Swindon lay principally in the hands of separate local boards of health for the two communities. These were established in 1864, and until the 1880s they were reluctant to collaborate with each other. Only in 1897 was the possibility seriously entertained of combining the two administrations as an incorporated borough, almost certainly in the hope that by the 1901 census the total population would exceed 50,000 and thus qualify Swindon for the status of a county borough. In the event this hope was not realized, but incorporation took place in 1900, and borough government continued until reorganization in 1974. From 1902 Swindon was also an autonomous education authority for most purposes.

The population continued to rise during most of the period 1901-51, but much more slowly. In 1951 it had reached 69,000. In the early decades of this century four-fifths of Swindon's male workforce were employed in the works or on the railways. It has been claimed that it was the largest industrial undertaking in Europe at the time. After 1925 the numbers employed began to decline, as rail traffic itself faced increasing competition from road vehicles. True suburban development, as opposed to the earlier speculative infilling around New Swindon of the later nineteenth century, accommodated the twentieth century increase, with ribbon development occurring in most directions, and a substantial northward boundary extension in 1928. Wartime brought an influx of new engineering and other industries, and temporarily swelled the population of the area. During and after the war the borough council devoted much effort to retaining and augmenting this welcome diversification, while at the same time attempting to improve living conditions and facilities for Swindon residents.

In this expansionary climate it is not surprising that an opportunity to receive London overspill population was enthusiastically pursued. A period of rapid growth ensued, with an annual population rise of about 3,000 between 1955 and 1963. By 1966 Swindon's population had reached 98,410, and the first phase of post-war expansion was complete. Plans during the 1960s for further massive expansion were later scaled down (a 400,000 population by the year 2000 was envisaged by consultants at one stage), but extensive developments have taken place on Swindon's eastern, western, and north-western flanks, with further development to come. The 1991 census for Swindon itself records a total population of 113,628, which would equate to nearly 150,000 if the entire urban area were included. Meanwhile the workforce of the railway works fell steadily during the 1960s, and was a mere 2,200 in 1973 (out of a borough total of manufacturing jobs of some 35,000). By 1986, when the works closed, office-based employment and work in emerging 'hi-tech' industries had become the dominant sources of new jobs.

The Great Western Railway's decision to build its railway works in rural countryside had obvious demographic implications. Even if surplus labour had been available locally a skilled workforce would have had to be recruited from areas with an engineering tradition. The first employees included men from Dundee, Merseyside, the Bristol area, and a considerable number from Tyneside. The 1851 census reveals that fewer than one-half the population of New Swindon (including children) were Wiltshire natives. Successive commentators observed that the attitudes and lifestyles of these newcomers were vastly different from those of the labourers in the surrounding countryside. They were in general independent, lively, and spendthrift, enjoying better education and higher wages than their country neighbours. These social differences continued and increased through the nineteenth and into the twentieth century, creating a basic tension between town and country which may be traced to the present day.

In the nineteenth century one of its manifestations was the prolonged hostility between Old and New Swindons, and the operation of separate local boards. A suggestion in 1878 that old jealousies were dying out proved premature, and amalgamation only came after the physical coalescence of the two towns, in 1900. It is noticeable that the change of heart followed recognition that Swindon might thereby achieve county borough status, thus freeing the two urban districts (as the boards became in 1894) from the authority of a new common enemy, the Wiltshire County Council (formed in 1888). However, each time renewed attempts were made to secure this prized status, in 1914, 1945 and 1966, they were thwarted by circumstances beyond Swindon's control. Nevertheless a degree of autonomy not enjoyed by other local authorities within Wiltshire was achieved by Swindon in the fields not only of education, but also justice (1906, 1962), health (1946) and planning (from 1948).

Political and financial tensions between the three local authorities involved - Swindon Borough Council, Wiltshire County Council, and Highworth Rural District Council - surfaced during the debate in 1952 and 1959 over London overspill expansion. Highworth RDC in 1947 had refused an offer to employ jointly with Swindon a planning officer to oversee post-war development, and had opposed the new estate at Penhill. Wiltshire County Council, prompted by the agricultural lobby, and suspecting that Swindon's motive in wishing to expand was to secure county borough status, opposed and then reluctantly acceded to watered-down expansion plans. A study of Swindon's planning history (by J.B. Harloe) has concluded that: 'The possibility that Swindon would encroach on the surrounding rural areas was at the heart of the opposition to the town's growth. After the first few years, the rural district councils did not oppose new industry and private housing being developed in their areas. However they did not want to lose their political independence and face the prospect of increased rates if parts of their areas were included within the borough boundary. In a county dominated by rural interests, their views had more impact on the County Council than Swindon's claims. It is hardly surprising that for many years the town's activities were viewed with a distinct air of disapproval from County Hall.'

Historical data, contemporary opinion, and more recent studies appear unanimous in presenting the Swindon which has emerged since 1840 as quite different from the rest of Wiltshire. A social and cultural identity distinct from that of the county was established during the nineteenth century, and flavoured the activities of the borough council established in 1900 with a progressive and independent civic pride. Expansion after 1952 created a third Swindon, with a new social mixture and a greatly enlarged boundary, which generated further friction between the town and its country cousins. At the 1971 census 83% of the population of the Highworth RDC area lived in the seven parishes which adjoined Swindon (including 40% in Stratton St Margaret and 17% in Wroughton) so that the amalgamation of Swindon Borough and Highworth RDC at local government reorganization in 1974 was a logical step. As Thamesdown Borough Council this authority continued the policies and traits which we have identified in Swindon, and elements of the old antipathy between town and county remained, right up until the divorce was made absolute with the formation of a unitary authority, Swindon Borough Council, in April 1997.

Swindon and its surrounding suburbs and villages will, it is hoped, continue to be regarded (on both sides of the new boundary) as part of the historical county and geographical region which has been Wiltshire for over a millennium. Indeed, now that the festering tensions have been alleviated by Swindon's new status, there should be many opportunities for friendly and productive co-operation. As a regional centre, too, and service provider over a considerable area, Swindon will continue to be a significant factor in the social and commercial life of the new county of Wiltshire from which it has been removed.

2 A Sense of Community

GOVERNMENT STATISTICS begin with Domesday Book, 1086. Like that even earlier census, the Biblical decree of Caesar Augustus, Domesday was concerned with revenue and tax. It stands at the head of a great series of medieval and later taxation records which, although incomplete and ambiguous, provide historians with some of their most important statistical information. The church, too, maintained lists of inhabitants from 1538 onwards, in the form of parish registers of baptisms, marriages, and burials, and in 1676 undertook an enquiry into religious adherence, conformist and nonconformist, which was known as the Compton Census. Soon afterwards, in 1695, the government held the first national population census, in connection with a marriage duty tax. Most of its results are lost, though in Wiltshire lists survive of inhabitants in the Swindon and Wootton Bassett area, and for Donhead, which can be connected with it.

Interest in demography was renewed in the late-18th century, under the influence of the theories of population increase propounded by Thomas Malthus, and this led in 1801 to the first of the decennial censuses which (except in 1941) have been held ever since. From 1841 onwards data have been collected about individuals – name, age, position in families, occupation, and parish of birth – and subjected to increasingly more sophisticated analysis in the published reports. In 1851 the census was arranged by registration districts, which were themselves based on the new poor law unions. All subsequent censuses have supplied the various agencies of local government, including sanitary districts, urban and rural districts, counties and parishes, with statistics relating to their areas.

The value of reliable demographic information, therefore, was recognized by Victorian administrators, who were concerned particularly with improving the sanitary condition of towns, and – to that end – the regulation of new housing. Between the wars faltering steps were taken to introduce forward planning policies, and these led to the first major legislation in this area, the 1947 Town and Country Planning Act. Councils were required to undertake surveys and prepare development plans, which would include maps showing the areas intended for particular land uses. Wiltshire's development plan was eventually approved in 1959, and subsequently amended. A new planning act was passed in 1968, and this laid emphasis for the first time on 'strategic' planning, and the production of 'structure' plans. In order to draw up such plans surveys had to be undertaken into the principal physical and economic characteristics of the area and, where relevant, neighbouring areas as well. Following local government reorganization in 1974 Wiltshire County Council began work on producing three structure plans, to cover south, north-east, and western Wiltshire. They were complemented by local plans prepared by the five new district councils for towns and areas within their jurisdiction.

The reports of survey for the three structure plans (which together covered the whole of Wiltshire, including Swindon), were published in 1978/9, and each included a chapter on population. Statistics were drawn from the most recent decennial census, that of 1971, supplemented by estimates derived from electoral registers, school rolls, child health records, and other sources. The philosophy behind this demographic analysis was expressed in the following terms:

> An examination of the changing size and characteristics of an area's population is central to the preparation of a structure plan. It provides a basis for estimating future demand for jobs, housing and services and for assessing the implications of the development pressures caused by this demand. The importance of population change to planning policies can only be appreciated fully by exploring the impact of change in the size, distribution and components of population upon the area's economy, housing stock, services, and environment.

In addition to their value for strategic planning, demographic data began to be used to address other local government issues. In 1974 the County Council's Social Services Department issued a booklet of graphs and tables entitled *Wiltshire Basic Data*. This presented for the county as a whole, and for the four districts for which the department was responsible (excluding Thamesdown), population vital statistics, and details of occupations, housing, car ownership, and rural isolation. It was revised in 1980, using headcount data collected in 1978 by the Planning Department, who had sent out a simple questionnaire to all householders with the electoral registration form. The County Council has also monitored changes in other aspects relevant to the structure plans. Since the late 1970s, annual surveys of housing development and the housing market, and employment development, have been published. Surveys of rural facilities, which had begun in 1964, were repeated in 1976, 1983, and thereafter at approximately three-yearly intervals, most recently in 1997. They are carried out by the County Council in conjunction with parish councils, and cover topics such as village shops and post offices, commercial premises, petrol stations, recreation grounds, public transport, schools, and miscellaneous facilities, such as churches, village halls, doctors' surgeries, phone boxes and mobile library stops.

Following submission and approval of the three county structure plans, a rolling programme of monitoring them was continued throughout the 1980s, and revised plans were approved in 1990 and 1993. A further review of the structure plans is now in hand, with some joint working between Wiltshire County and Swindon Borough Councils. Since 1989 population reviews and projections have been published, together with a wider ranging document, *County Trends*. This aimed to set out in easily accessible form the main trends affecting the County Council as a whole, and specific services, over the ensuing twelve years. The most recent issue, published in 1993, took backward and forward views, from 1981 to 2002, and included projections for population and demography, housing and households, economy and employment, social class, car availability, traffic and commuting. By the time that this book is published a new 1998 edition of *County Trends* will be available.

Each decennial census refines its data collection, so that the results of the 1991 census are more sophisticated than any of its predecessors. Small area statistics can be purchased from the Office for National Statistics for areas known as enumeration districts. These are the areas for which a single enumerator was responsible for collecting the census data, and can be used to define larger areas such as parishes or electoral wards. For each enumeration district some 10,000 individual items of data are provided in about 90 different tables, although responses to some of the questions asked by the census are only made available as a 10% sample. The result is a powerful tool for research and analysis, which local authorities can use in a variety of ways.

With the focusing on the nineteen community areas described in this book as the basis for service provision in the new Wiltshire, the 1991 census data are being analysed to give profiles for each community. In June 1996 Wiltshire County Council issued a provisional volume of profiles for all the communities, and subsequently a separate document for each has been produced. These include comparative data, for the individual community and for the new county as a whole, relating to population, employment, income, travel, and education. Further topics, such as dwellings, rural facilities and land use, are planned. The statistical profiles have been used to contribute to the thumbnail portraits of each community presented in Chapter 3, and to construct the matrix or 'league table' of communities given as an appendix to Chapter 3.

3 Wiltshire Communities

Introduction

THIS CHAPTER examines each of the nineteen community areas into which the new Wiltshire has been divided. We shall look at them in the light of the information which we described in Chapters 1 and 2, considering not only the physical appearance of their landscapes, but also the settlement patterns of their towns and villages, the social profile of their populations, and the validity of the boundaries which have been drawn around them, both in terms of their history and their current relevance. Information about each community is presented in exactly the same way, so as to make comparisons between them straightforward.

Malmesbury

IN WILTSHIRE'S north-western corner, the Malmesbury community area shares the Cotswold scenery of its neighbour, Gloucestershire, especially around Sherston and Malmesbury itself. Further east, around Minety, is thinly-populated clayland, part of the former forest of Bradon, and here several large tracts of woodland remain. Dauntsey, the area's southernmost parish, occupies a wide clayland valley, Dauntsey Vale, now crossed by the M4 motorway. Dividing the two geological regions, Oolitic limestone to the west, Oxford clay to the east, is the valley formed by the southward-flowing River (Bristol) Avon, whose headwaters meet at Malmesbury. The river is augmented by streams flowing into it near the Somerfords from east (Brinkworth Brook) and west (Gauze Brook). Crudwell, Oaksey, and Minety, along the area's northern edge, are drained by the Swill Brook, a tributary of the Thames.

Ready supply of good limestone, for walls and roofs, has given most building in the area its Cotswold character, and this is well seen in the only town, Malmesbury, which occupies a dramatic and picturesque site within a meander of the Avon. Despite its urban feel, and closebuilt historic centre with a good range of basic shopping and other facilities, Malmesbury's population, at around 4,700, is small, and residents of the area rely also on Chippenham, Cirencester, and Swindon as service providers. Sherston, the area's most populous village, once enjoyed urban status, albeit on a very modest scale, and still acts as a focus for the Cotswold villages around it. Minety and Brinkworth have experienced recent growth, and with Sherston and six other settlements in the area enjoy basic village facilities. Dispersed substantial farmhouses and minor roadside hamlets are scattered throughout the area, between the more substantial nucleated villages, such as Great Somerford, Luckington and Crudwell.

The area is among the wealthiest in Wiltshire, with more cars per household than any other, and the second highest average income (after Downton). It has a high proportion of qualified males, and of long-distance commuting (the M4 Junction 17 is readily accessible), coupled with a low unemployment rate. Away from the chalkland communities it has the largest area, but is relatively sparsely populated, although most other population characteristics fall within the middle of the range for Wiltshire as a whole.

The boundaries of the community area follow those of the pre-1974 Malmesbury RDC and its antecedents, the poor law union, rural sanitary and highway districts. They correspond quite closely also to Malmesbury's sphere of influence, as assessed in 1950, its secondary school catchment area drawn in 1946, and the coverage of its local trade directory published between the wars. The poor law union incorporated most of the ancient Malmesbury hundred, to which were added Sherston and its neighbours (originally the medieval hundred of Dunlow). Malmesbury hundred was in turn related to, and greatly influenced by, Malmesbury Abbey, which, by a series of acquisitions during the Saxon and medieval periods, came to control most of the settlements within it. Until the 19th century one parish in the community area, Minety, was administratively a detached portion of Gloucestershire, and several border parishes, formerly in Malmesbury hundred, were transferred from Wiltshire to Gloucestershire in 1896 (Kemble and Poole Keynes) and 1930 (Ashley and Long Newnton).

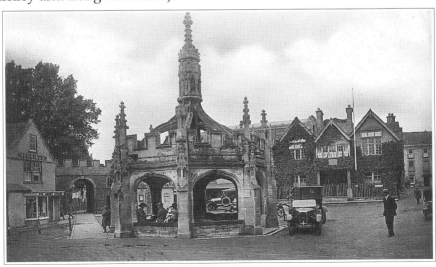

Wootton Bassett

THIS PREDOMINANTLY clayland community area extends from the Upper Thames Valley and Gloucestershire border in the north, to the greensand escarp-ment which defines the edge of the Marlborough Downs at Clyffe Pypard and Broad Town in the south. Across the area runs the ridge of Corallian limestone which separates the Oxford clay of the former Bradon Forest around Purton and the Lydiards, from the Kimmeridge clay at Tockenham and Bushton. Lyneham airfield and Wootton Bassett are built on this ridge, which also provides a rough building stone (ragstone) for the area. Cricklade stands at a historic crossing of the Thames, and large-scale extraction of Thames gravels upstream around Ashton Keynes has created a landscape of lakes known as the Cotswold Water Park. Some of these lakes are exploited for leisure purposes, while others are important wildlife reserves. North of Cricklade the villages of Latton and Marston Maisey, together with their neighbours (now in the Swindon authority) are characteristic Cotswold settlements of the Cirencester region.

Wootton Bassett (around 11,000 population) and Cricklade (now over 4,000) are both historic towns with a range of shopping and other facilities, but their proximity to Swindon dwarfs them as urban centres, and to a major extent they serve as commuter dormitories to the Swindon conurbation and (via the M4 junctions 15 and 16) to places further afield. Purton, Lydiard Millicent, and Ashton Keynes are substantial villages with basic facilities, and Lyneham (with a population of about 5,700) is an important air force establishment. The Lydiards have lost portions of their historic territory to Swindon's western housing expansion during the 1980s. Elsewhere the area displays the typical clayland pattern of small villages, roadside hamlets, and isolated farms.

The community area is of average size for Wiltshire, but with a relatively high population and population density. Car ownership and average income are both very high, with low unemployment, but a less qualified than average workforce, and relatively little long-distance commuting. The rate of housebuilding experienced during the 1970s and 1980s has now slackened, and only modest population growth is projected, with little inward migration but a high birthrate; although further development is possible following local and structure plan reviews.

The antecedents of the community area boundaries are the pre-1974 Cricklade and Wootton Bassett RDC, which was based on a poor law union created in 1834. The western boundary, despite its ragged appearance, is much more ancient, since it separated medieval hundreds and rural deaneries. But Cricklade and Wootton Bassett have only been bedfellows since 1834 – the earlier hundred groupings allied Cricklade with Highworth, and Wootton Bassett with Swindon. Wootton Bassett and the southern parishes of the community area formed part of Swindon highway district in 1864, while Cricklade and the northern parishes had their own separate district. Since the 19th century proximity to (and distancing from) Swindon have been the unifying factors for the towns and villages within this community area, rather than any deep-seated affiliation to each other.

TOWN HALL, WOOTTON BASSETT.

Chippenham

THE BRISTOL AVON flows southwards in its broad and undramatic valley through the claylands along the eastern edge of Chippenham community area, and Chippenham itself was established in one of the river's many meanders. Westward from Chippenham the landscape becomes more broken, taking on the typical Cotswold scenery of deep valleys and flatter high plains. Castle Combe, hiding in the dramatic By Brook Valley, is the most memorable of several handsome limestone villages, which include also Yatton Keynell and Kington St Michael. Communications run east-west across the area, the M4 motorway (with junctions north of Chippenham and at Tormarton, just beyond the boundary with South Gloucestershire to the west) replacing the old main road (A420) from Bristol to Chippenham, which then continued via Christian Malford and Sutton Benger towards Swindon. The potential growth in importance of the A350 north-south route, and its western by-pass of the town, are seen by both County and District authorities as a key to economic development in western Wiltshire.

Chippenham itself, which accounted in 1991 for nearly 80% of the total population, dominates the area, and is the only town. Its population has doubled since the 1960s, and it vies with Trowbridge to be the second largest town in the new Wiltshire (after Salisbury). Castle Combe, historically speaking, is an industrial medieval town, but its modern accolade of 'prettiest village in England' has fossilized it as a tourist attraction. Its neighbouring villages and hamlets in the Cotswold west of the area look to Bristol and Bath as much as to Chippenham. Elsewhere, Sutton Benger, Christian Malford, and Kington St Michael are medium-sized villages with basic facilities and, with Kington Langley and other smaller settlements north of Chippenham, have become popular because of their proximity to the motorway junction.

In terms of population Chippenham is the largest community area in Wiltshire, although geographically it is only of average size, and away from the town and its suburbs it is quite sparsely populated. Its 1990s population increase (actual and projected), birthrate, inward migration, and housebuilding, are all the highest in Wiltshire, emphasizing Chippenham's strategic position and perceived suitability for major housing and employment development. The average income of its residents, percentage of qualified males, and commuting activity, are all above the Wiltshire average as well, but the number of cars per household is low, the number of qualified working women the lowest in Wiltshire, and unemployment is about average.

The boundaries of Chippenham and Corsham community areas, taken together, correspond to those of a poor law union established in 1834, a highway district, and the Chippenham RDC, until its merger with Calne RDC in 1934. The Chippenham poor law union was itself based on the territories of two medieval hundreds, Chippenham and North Damerham (together with Seagry and Stanton St Quinton, from Malmesbury hundred). Chippenham community area's eastern boundary (with Calne) is ancient, since it divided not only hundreds, but also medieval deaneries. With the Corsham area removed the resulting Chippenham community has a ragged shape, but all its settlements are readily accessible by the main roads which radiate from the town.

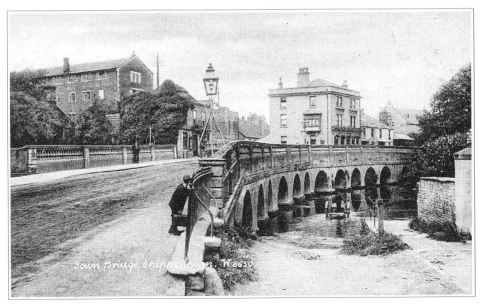

Town Bridge, Chippenham. W.8650.

Corsham

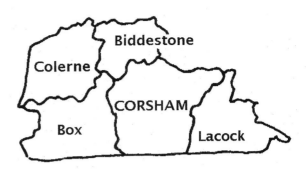

APART FROM LACOCK, which straddles the valley of the Bristol Avon, the Corsham community area lies entirely on the Oolitic and Inferior limestones of the southern Cotswolds. Indeed the freestones mined and quarried at Box and Corsham have been the mainstay of its economy and its principal claim to fame. Despite its insignificant appearance, the By Brook has carved a deep and picturesque valley between Box and Colerne, isolating Colerne and Slaughterford from the rest of the area. Corsham and Box are linked with Chippenham to the east and Bath to the west by the main A4 Bath Road, giving the area easy access and a close affiliation to Bath.

The area comprises just five large parishes, of which two – Biddestone and Colerne – are centred on attractive Cotswold villages. Historically, Lacock and Corsham are small towns which grew up beside major houses, Lacock Abbey and Corsham Court, but Lacock's stagnation since the eighteenth century (when the line of the Bath Road through it was diverted elsewhere) has turned it into a fossilized tourist attraction. At Corsham, however, and its neighbour Box (which has never had urban aspirations) the winning of stone has resulted in a scattered pattern of older cottage settlements, which infilling by modern housing has tended to coalesce. These two parishes in 1996 had a combined population of nearly 15,000, more than three-quarters of the area total. The growth of the area's population was stimulated during and after the second world war by the naval use of disused stone mines (at Copenacre and Rudloe, for instance), and by an important military airfield at Colerne.

The community area, in terms of population, birth and death rates, average income, and car ownership, stands in the middle of the range of Wiltshire communities. Because it is small in terms of area, the population density is accordingly quite high. Its working population includes a greater than average proportion of qualified men, and the highest proportion of qualified women of any area, but unemployment is also above average.

Historically, as we have seen, the Corsham area formed part of administrative units based on Chippenham. The distinct character of Corsham, Box, and their neighbours was recognized by 1851, when four of the five parishes (not Lacock) were grouped as a registration sub-district; and their cultural identity is seen too in the activities of Victorian carriers, school catchment areas, and shopping patterns. The influence of the old line of the Bath road, through Lacock, Corsham, and part of Box parish, may help to explain the area's strong affiliation with Bath. The straight southern boundary, which follows the line of a now vanished Roman road, has been observed by medieval hundreds and deaneries, as well as by all Victorian and more recent local government units, including Parliamentary constituencies.

Calne

ON THE MAP the community area based on Calne is the most regular of all, nearly circular and with its town dead centre. On the ground matters are not so simple. The eastern and

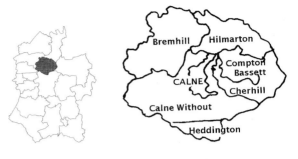

south-eastern fringe, from Yatesbury past Cherhill and Calstone to Heddington, forms the western edge of the Marlborough Downs, high chalkland which culminates in two of the great landmarks of central Wiltshire, Oldbury Camp above Cherhill, with its white horse and monument, and Morgans Hill above Calstone, with its twin radio masts. Calne itself sits in the valley beneath, beside a minor river, the Marden, near the junction of the Gault and Kimmeridge clays, the greensand, and the Coral rag. The Corallian ridge runs north past Bremhill and Hilmarton to Lyneham airfield, but southwards it is mantled by the greensand. Both outcrops make for interesting, undulating scenery, which has been modified to memorable effect by the creation of Bowood Park, west of Calne.

Calne is a town of contrasts, elegant houses around its green and along its older streets, but cheek-by-jowl with nondescript modern buildings and dreary suburbs, an interminable ribbon development along the main road eastwards as far as Quemerford, and a grassed open space where its famous bacon factory was demolished during the 1980s. This plucking-out of the town's industrial heart has been followed by a regeneration programme – the Calne Project – which is now bearing fruit. Away from the town geology has affected the settlement pattern, with compact but remote villages – Calstone, Yatesbury, Heddington – on the chalk, two substantial elongated villages – Compton Bassett and Cherhill – beneath the escarpment, dispersed hamlets on the clays and ragstone of Bremhill and Hilmarton parishes, and picturesque estate villages around the edge of Bowood, at Derry Hill and Sandy Lane. The area's great variety is seen in microcosm within a single parish, Hilmarton, which boasts a Victorian estate village (Hilmarton itself), a dispersed and straggling hamlet (Goatacre), two tiny chalkland settlements (Highway and Clevancy), and an assortment of isolated clayland farms.

The Calne area's vital statistics, of population, birth and death rates, hectarage, population density, car ownership, average income, and proportion of qualified males, all place it near the middle of the range of Wiltshire communities. The increase in its population between 1991 and 2001 is projected to be the second highest in Wiltshire in percentage terms, exceeded only by its neighbour Chippenham, although it has to be said that actual housebuilding rates have been much lower than those previously forecast. Its proportion of qualified working women is lower than any other area except Chippenham.

The area's boundaries are those of the 1834 poor law union which later became Calne RDC (merged with Chippenham RDC in 1934). Most of the southern and eastern boundaries are also those of Calne hundred, and so are probably ancient. The eastern half of the area's boundary, in fact, bordering Wootton Bassett, Marlborough, and part of Devizes communities, scores as very highly or highly significant, whereas the ragged boundary with Chippenham to the west, across the ancient no-man's-land of the former Pewsham Forest, is far less distinct. From the maps of spheres of influence it seems clear that Calne's hinterland has always been small, squeezed by Chippenham and Devizes, and more recently by Swindon, and that its limits (as seen, for example, by the school catchment area) correspond closely with those of the community area.

Marlborough

THE LARGEST GEOGRAPHICALLY, Marlborough community area has three characteristic types of scenery. Tracts of typical chalk downland along its northern and south-western edges (the Marlborough Downs) rise to some of the highest points in Wiltshire, with noble views over Pewsey Vale and the north Wiltshire claylands. Between the downs runs the course of the River Kennet southward (seldom now - sadly - flowing in its upper reaches), from its source near Broad Hinton, via Avebury, where it turns east, then Marlborough and Ramsbury, to Chilton Foliat, where it leaves Wiltshire for Berkshire and, ultimately, the Thames. South of Marlborough, on the flinty soils overlying the chalk, is Savernake Forest, sheltering its scattering of woodland-edge settlements, of which Great Bedwyn is the most notable.

Marlborough itself, with its broad High Street and sloping Green dressed in their Sunday-best architecture, is the only town. Its shops are a cut above, as is its best-known institution, Marlborough College, which claims many famous alumni. The Victorian public school replaced the dwindling stagecoach trade and restored the town's prosperity; indeed the school's nucleus was a coaching inn, and others still line the High Street. Only four villages in the area attain more than a thousand inhabitants. Burbage, spread along and behind a now by-passed main street, and Aldbourne, memorably ranged about a green and pond, are true villages. Ramsbury, once home to Wiltshire's bishops and cathedral, and Great Bedwyn, an erstwhile borough, have had urban aspirations in the past. Except in Savernake, where settlement is scattered, most of the communities' villages border the Kennet, or its minor tributary the Og, with their parishes extending up the hillside and on to the downs. Of these the best known and most visited is Avebury, an atmospheric place of hikers, wholefood, and megalithic enigma.

Because it is so large, the Marlborough community area's population density is relatively low, despite a total population above the average of Wiltshire communities. The predicted increase in population 1991-2001, inward migration, and new housebuilding, are all slightly above average, with slightly less than average unemployment. Car ownership and average income are high, with a large proportion of qualified working men, and a high incidence of long-distance commuting.

Although the ancestry of the Marlborough and Ramsbury RDC, with which this community is nearly coterminous, is the Marlborough Poor Law Union joined to the Wiltshire portion of the Hungerford Union, the territory of the resulting hybrid is in sympathy with the region's topography, since, apart from the loss of the Shalbourne area to the Tidworth community, it coincides almost exactly with the Wiltshire watersheds of the River Kennet. The community boundaries mirror even more closely the Marlborough Highway District, established in 1864, which (unlike the unions and rural districts) sensibly linked Burbage with Marlborough rather than Pewsey. The community's north-western boundary, along the chalk escarpment of the Marlborough Downs, seems to be one of the most significant in Wiltshire.

Bradford on Avon

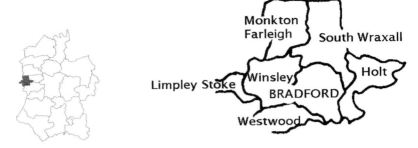

AFTER URBAN SALISBURY, Bradford is the smallest community in area, and consists of just the town itself, five adjoining parishes, and Limpley Stoke, which juts into former Somerset. It lies at the southern end of Wiltshire's limestone belt, and yielded only to Box and Corsham in the quality of its freestone quarries and mines. Limestone, and modern imitations, are near universal in the area's buildings, and combine with the understated ruggedness of Cotswold scenery to produce handsome, comfortable landscapes. The Limpley Stoke valley, formed by the Avon along the county's western boundary, is justly praised.

The town of Bradford, like its neighbours Melksham, Trowbridge, and Westbury, was founded on clothmaking, and former mills, clothiers' houses, and weavers' cottages remain. What distinguishes Bradford, and makes it so attractive, is its setting, perched on its hillside overlooking the river and its great bridge. It enjoys a vigorous, loyal, and somewhat idiosyncratic sense of community; and it occupies a position, socially as well as geographically, somewhere between Trowbridge and Bath. Of its satellite villages – historically members of the greater Bradford — Winsley, Westwood, and Holt have considerable dormitory populations, while retaining (Holt especially) strong community identities of their own. South Wraxall, Monkton Farleigh, and Limpley Stoke are smaller and their populations more scattered.

In terms of population Bradford is the fourth lowest of the Wiltshire communities, although its density within so small an area is very high. Its predicted population change 1991-2001 is the lowest of any community, with a low birthrate, and comparatively little new housebuilding or inward migration. It has the highest proportion of qualified working men in Wiltshire, with a correspondingly high average income, but also high unemployment. Car ownership is above average, but relatively few Bradfordians commute long distances.

Bradford's northern and western boundaries, a former Roman road and the county border respectively, are ancient. But to reflect the hundred and union based on Bradford, the community area should have been drawn considerably larger, to include Wingfield, Atworth, and Broughton Gifford, and so in the south and east the boundaries have no historical validity. Nevertheless, the community area as it has been agreed does approximate to the map of shopping areas in 1950, and is perhaps an accurate reflection of Bradford's historic sphere of influence.

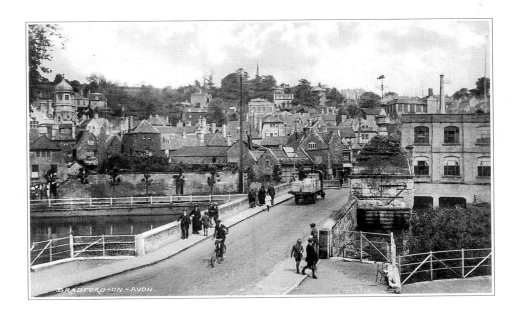

Melksham

LIKE ITS NEIGHBOUR Bradford, Melksham is a very small community area with a relatively large population. The Corallian ridge defines its eastern edge, and to the west the area extends on to the limestone, with the result that mellow stonebuilt houses abound in Broughton Gifford and Atworth, and in the town centre of Melksham itself. But most of Melksham – the urban area and its extensive 'Without' parish – sit on clay bisected by the River Avon. Indeed, the impression gained from neighbouring high ground, the Ridge above Whitley or Bowden Hill above Lacock, is of a 'city of the plain', housing estates and industrial premises which have been caught in a web of cables spun from giant electricity pylons.

Melksham's reputation as the least attractive of the Wiltshire clothmaking towns is reinforced by the industrial setting of the main Chippenham to Warminster road (the A350), from which most outsiders gain their first impression. Clothmaking was replaced by rubber, electrical, and dairy processing industries, which brought not only unsightly factories but also nondescript housing estates. But the kernel of Melksham, Canonhold around the church, the Kings Arms and the market place, parts of the High Street and Lowbourne, are as good as most comparable towns and better than many. Housing extends southward along the tedious main road; eastwards, beyond the solid houses of a failed spa, to cover a former airfield, Bower Hill; and north-eastwards to the edge of the former Melksham Forest. North and west of the Avon the villages appear to have more in common with neighbouring areas. Beanacre, Shaw and Whitley have the feel of Corsham, while Atworth and Broughton Gifford (with its memorable common-edge houses) seem more in tune with the Bradford and Bath countryside.

Melksham's population is above average for Wiltshire communities, and because its area is small, the population density is third highest in the county, after Salisbury and Trowbridge. Although predicted population growth is in the middle of the range, more new houses and inward migration than for most communities are anticipated up to 2001. Car ownership is average, but there is relatively little long distance commuting and a below average proportion of qualified males. By contrast the rate of qualified working women is exceeded only by its neighbour, Corsham. The average income is the lowest in Wiltshire.

The community area's straight northern boundary is the line of a former Roman road, which has always formed an administrative boundary from the medieval hundred and rural deanery onwards. None of the other boundaries have much historical validity, since Seend, Hilperton, Trowbridge, and Semington have all in the past been grouped with Melksham, whereas Atworth and Broughton Gifford owed their allegiance to Bradford. But, as in the case of Bradford, the area's boundaries as drawn do correspond quite well with the shopping patterns mapped in 1950, and so may reflect Melksham's historic sphere of influence.

Trowbridge

THE MAIN ROAD on its way north from Westbury to Melksham climbs on to the Corallian ridge between Yarnbrook and West Ashton, bisecting Trowbridge's community area. The long view westwards from the road reveals Trowbridge itself in the clay vale, characterized by warehouses, its church spire, and the remaining chimneys of former cloth mills. The view beyond the town is darkened by distant woodland, remnants of the great Selwood Forest which divided Wiltshire from Somerset. East of the road is the territory of Steeple Ashton, and beyond it Keevil, still essentially clayland, but here punctuated by the ragstone ridge, and running up to the chalk escarpment beyond. From the road the area seems sparsely populated, as indeed parts of it are, but this impression is misleading. For, urban Salisbury apart, Trowbridge has the densest concentration of population in the new Wiltshire.

The status of Trowbridge as county town, a surprise to many outsiders, is not based on historical importance, but on Victorian expediency – it was accessible by rail from the north, centre, and south of Wiltshire. It is a workaday town, depending not only on county and district officialdom, but also on meat and dairy products, bedding, cosmetics, a host of smaller industries, and a thriving commercial centre. Recent growth has encroached on Hilperton, Staverton, and North Bradley, which have themselves developed as dormitory suburbs. The area's clothmaking heritage is apparent not only in Trowbridge itself, with its former cloth mills and clothiers' houses (some of the grandest Georgian architecture in any Wiltshire town), but also in the common-edge settlements of small-scale domestic weaving, at Southwick, Wingfield, and North Bradley. By contrast Keevil and Steeple Ashton, to the east of the area, are picturesque villages – the latter a former small town with a noble church and a large rural hinterland – but the affluence of their showpiece buildings was also acquired from clothmaking, in its pre-industrial phase.

Although relatively compact, Trowbridge is the third most populous community area, after Chippenham and Salisbury, and its anticipated population increase to 2001, new housebuilding, and inward migration, are all also the third highest. The town itself has experienced considerable economic change, with the decline in traditional industries being offset more recently by the growth of new ones in locations such as the White Horse Business Park. The proportion of qualified working adults lies in the middle of the range, but car ownership is low, with most of the workforce commuting short distances, and the lowest incidence of long-distance commuting of any area. Average income is relatively low, and the unemployment rate is the highest in Wiltshire.

Except along the western border with Somerset, and part of the southern border with Westbury and Heywood, no appeal to traditional boundaries can sensibly be made to establish the community area around Trowbridge. Anciently the town and parish lay within Melksham hundred, and the 1834 poor law union boundary perpetuated this. But Trowbridge had outgrown this subordinate position, and a local board of health was established in 1864, leading to an urban sanitary district and UDC. Unlike other Wiltshire towns, however, Trowbridge had no RDC to govern its hinterland, which was split between Bradford, Melksham, and Westbury. The community boundaries as drawn in fact reflect the more limited spheres of influence of the neighbouring towns, since because of its size and importance Trowbridge has for many purposes established itself as the centre of a larger community which subsumes them.

Westbury

 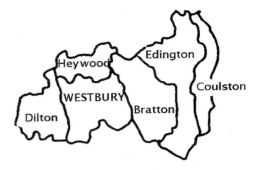

WESTBURY-UNDER-THE-PLAYNE, as it was sometimes known, must have aptly described the little town, established at the foot of the great domed chalk escarpment which can be seen from half of Wiltshire and most of northeast Somerset. The Westbury community area, although fourth smallest geographically, embraces a diversity of scenery. Running east from the town towards Devizes the elongated springline parishes of Bratton, Edington (with Tinhead), and Coulston each have their feet in the low, flat clay, their midriffs cut into the greensand, and their heads high on the desolate military downland. But from Westbury itself, running west to the Somerset boundary, the geological outcrops becomes more confused, from chalk to greensand, gault and clay, and the scenery less predictable. Flat pastures alternate with intricate and secretive valleys, and wooded hillsides. Waterfilled pits near the railway station are the legacy of an industry not usually associated with Wiltshire, the extraction of iron ore. Inextricably tethered to the county, by contrast, the docile white horse stands sentinel on the hillside overlooking Westbury.

A clothmaking town like its neighbours, Westbury retains its gargantuan Angel and Bitham Mills near its centre, and informal weavers' settlements on the former wastes and commons at Westbury Leigh and Dilton Marsh. It was also a Parliamentary borough, and still gives its name to west Wiltshire's constituency. Its compact market square, presided over by squat town hall and sprawling inn next-door, seems tailor-made for declaring the results of corrupt 18th-century elections. An important railway junction, the town has expanded westwards towards its station and the long-established trading estate, as well as southwards, to engulf Westbury Leigh in suburban bungalows, and now northwards, with starter homes facing Trowbridge. Away from the town to the east, Westbury's area has two large villages, Bratton and Edington, with their own strong sense of community, the former (historically) a centre of nonconformity, the latter renowned for its priory church and annual music festival. West of Westbury, beyond the railway tracks at Brokerswood and Brook, is an almost inaccessible pocket of Wiltshire where hardly anybody lives.

Although Westbury's population total is below the average for Wiltshire communities, density is relatively high, and the anticipated increase to 2001, with corresponding inward migration and new housebuilding, are all above average. Incomes, the proportion of qualified working adults, and of car ownership, are all towards the middle of the range, with more local than long-distance commuting, and a much higher than average unemployment rate.

Westbury was the centre of a hundred which included also Heywood, Bratton, and Dilton (and half of Chapmanslade), so that, apart from Edington and Coulston, which were anciently allied to Steeple Ashton, the community area perpetuates ancient boundaries. Coulston was part of Edington parish, and its boundary with Erlestoke seems to have been significant; Edington, like Bratton, is closer and more accessible to Westbury along the scarp-foot road than to the towns of any of the neighbouring communities (a fact reflected, too, in its school catchment area), and so its inclusion in the Westbury community makes common-sense.

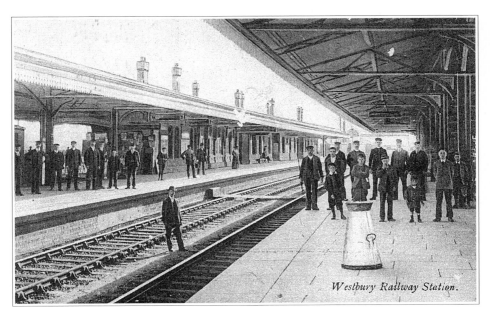

Westbury Railway Station.

Devizes

CLOSE TO WILTSHIRE'S
CENTRE, Devizes stands at
the western head of
Pewsey Vale, the valley
formed by the head-
waters of the Salisbury
or Christchurch Avon.
Around Devizes itself, and in the valley
floor running east, greensand outcrops, but to the north, above
Roundway, and to the south, above the Lavingtons, stand the rounded
chalk escarpments of the Marlborough Downs and Salisbury Plain
respectively. West of Devizes the landscape steps down on to the clay
vale of north and west Wiltshire, a transition symbolized by the Kennet
and Avon Canal's famous flight of locks at Caen Hill. Beyond the clay of
Poulshot, Worton, and Rowde, the Corallian ridge runs up the western
fringe of the area, here throwing up very fertile sandy soils around
Bromham, and ironstone at Seend. It is hard to better Thomas Fuller's
celebrated remark, published in 1661, praising the Devizes area, 'as
partaking of the pleasure of the plain, and the wealth of the deep country'.

After Salisbury, medieval Devizes created the largest hinterland of
any Wiltshire town, and its catchment area on market day still seems to
extend not only over its own community area, but also over much of
Pewsey's to the east. Its unusual town plan, curving around the Norman
castle which brought it into existence, has resulted in a pleasingly spacious
market place, which exudes on a sunny day a feeling of commercial self-
satisfaction and well-being. It shares a clothmaking tradition with the
west Wiltshire towns, and a stagecoaching past with Marlborough. Its
position at the centre of Wiltshire has made it the headquarters of many
countywide organizations, including the constabulary. Of the
surrounding villages only Market Lavington has ever aspired to be a
miniature town, and still has a greater range of services than elsewhere.
Potterne, Urchfont, Seend, and Bromham are all large villages, with
populations exceeding 1,000. Most of the other villages and hamlets are
compact and nucleated, after the chalkland fashion, though Worton and
Littleton Pannell (and Seend) have spread themselves along roads,
Poulshot around a large green, and Bromham and Bishops Cannings have

scattered farms away from their main centres.

The Devizes area is larger and considerably more populous than the average Wiltshire community, with one of the highest projected population increases to 2001, and a consequently high rate of inward migration and new dwellings. Average income and car ownership are in the middle of the range, but unemployment is high, despite an above-average proportion of qualified working women. There is, however, both recent and current commercial redevelopment of ex-army barrack sites on the north-east side of the town.

The community boundaries are broadly those of the pre-1974 Devizes RDC, except that Patney and Chirton have been placed with Pewsey. The RDC boundaries in turn conformed to the 1834 Devizes poor law union with the addition of Seend, acquired from Melksham. The union was an amalgamation of the ancient hundred of Potterne and Cannings, and the western half of Swanborough. Along its western and southern sides the community boundaries may be regarded as quite significant, and in the north the boundary between Bishops Cannings and Calne Without seems to be ancient and unchanging. The eastern boundary with Pewsey, wherever drawn, is open to criticism, because Devizes has always enjoyed a sphere of influence which includes most of Pewsey Vale. This is well seen by examining the routes of Victorian carriers, or the 1950 shopping patterns map. The agreed line has the virtues of creating two community areas of roughly similar size, and of recognizing that Stanton St Bernard, Patney, and Chirton all have more in common with their eastern than their western neighbours.

The Fountain, Market Place, Devizes.

Pewsey

Stanton St Bernard · Huish · Alton · Wilcot · Wootton Rivers · Milton · Lilborne · 1 · PEWSEY · Easton · Patney · 2 · N. Newnton · Chirton · Manningford · Marden · 3 · Upavon · 4 · Wilsford · Enford · Fittleton · Netheravon

1 Woodborough
2 Beechingstoke
3 Charlton
4 Rushall

THE TWO PRINCIPAL headwaters of the River Avon, flowing east from Bishops Cannings and west from Burbage along Pewsey Vale, meet at the centre of this community area, near Upavon, and flow south in a broad valley towards Amesbury. Apart from the parishes at its wide western end, the whole of Pewsey Vale is included, as well as the four most northerly parishes of the Avon valley. Along the floor of Pewsey Vale greensand outcrops, with occasional chalk outliers, such as Woodborough Hill and Picked Hill, but the greensand is everywhere framed by the gentle profiles of the chalk hills of the Marlborough Downs to the north, and the more severe escarpment of Salisbury Plain to the south. Those who settle in the Vale have their world defined for them by these chalk horizons. The Avon valley, which has cut its way south between the central and eastern blocks of Salisbury Plain, is like Pewsey Vale, but the hills are closer, and the river has grown to maturity. The south-western and south-eastern corners of the area extend across the menacing military wilderness of Salisbury Plain.

Pewsey, the eponymous capital of the vale, although invested with a certain status by virtue of its railway station, canal wharf, and minor administrative functions, is far from being a town. It has the largest population of any parish in the area (at about 3,000), and a range of shops and services, but for serious shopping people's loyalties have always been divided between Devizes to the west and Marlborough to the north. Upavon and Netheravon are large villages, but in this area, as across the chalklands, settlements tend to be small and compact, slightly raised above river level, and with strips of territory running from the valley floor to the high downs. The larger parishes, such as Enford or

Manningford, are amalgamations of several such villages or hamlets. The Kennet and Avon canal meanders its way unhurriedly along the Vale without a single lock.

The area's population total is the second smallest of any community (although set to increase between 1991 and 2001), and people are very thin on the ground. Average income and the incidence of car ownership are both very high, while the unemployment rate is low, and the area has the greatest proportion of long-distance commuters of any Wiltshire community.

Historically speaking, Pewsey never established a tangible sphere of influence around itself, so that the villages of this community area looked to Devizes or Marlborough, and in the upper Avon valley sometimes to Amesbury or Salisbury. It did, however, become the centre of a poor law union, and later a highway district and rural district, and the northern and southern boundaries of each were coterminous with those of the community area. The western boundary, with Devizes, has fluctuated, and the virtues of the present arrangement have already been discussed. Burbage, Everleigh, and parishes in the Tidworth area lay within Pewsey RDC, although the earlier union boundaries placed the line at the Collingbournes. The present division between Pewsey and Tidworth communities is based on no historical precedent, but on expediency, recognizing Tidworth's radically altered status during the present century.

PWY 22   HIGH STREET, PEWSEY.

Tidworth

EXCEPT AT SHALBOURNE AND HAM, this community area lies entirely on chalk, and its western edge from Tidworth to Everleigh is typical Salisbury Plain scenery, dominated by the forbidding profile of Sidbury Hill. East of the Collingbournes, and around Chute and Ludgershall, the chalk is mantled by flinty clay, and in consequence is heavily wooded. Beyond the woods, along the Hampshire border, is *terra incognita* to most Wiltshire people, a remote high chalkland ending abruptly at its northern end in a steep escarpment, below which Ham and Shalbourne shelter.

Ludgershall, historically speaking, is the most important settlement in the area, a miniature castle town and pocket borough, which became at the end of the 19th century the railhead for the army's advance on Salisbury Plain. One consequence of this advance was the creation, around and between two of the smaller villages, of the garrison town of Tidworth. Tidworth's population, depending on the vagaries of army postings, hovers around 9,000, more than twice that of Ludgershall, and considerably larger than Marlborough, but much of Tidworth has the feel of some home-counties suburb which has been towed away and moored on Salisbury Plain. Quite different are the Collingbournes, typical chalkland valley villages, or the woodland settlements of Chute and Chute Forest, or again the windswept downland villages of Tidcombe, Everleigh and Buttermere. And when we reach Shalbourne, well seen from the main road across its valley, or Ham, we begin to feel the pull of Berkshire and the Kennet valley.

Because Tidworth itself is dominated by service personnel, the area has an unusually youthful population profile, with many more births than deaths. Unemployment is very high, and incomes below average, for which the lowest proportion of qualified working males anywhere in Wiltshire may be partly to blame. Car ownership is correspondingly low.

Nearly half of this community's boundary is the county border with Hampshire and Berkshire, which has remained largely untouched for a millennium. However, acquisitions were made from Berkshire in the Shalbourne area during the 19th century, and South Tidworth and Faberstown (effectively part of Ludgershall) were transferred from Hampshire to Wiltshire in 1992. The poor law commissioners recognized the area's affinities beyond Wiltshire (which are still very valid), by placing the northern parishes in Hungerford union, and Tidworth, Ludgershall and the Chutes in the notorious Andover union. For county-based administration this was not possible, of course, and so the area was divided between Marlborough and Pewsey, two centres geographically remote from this special enclave of Wiltshire. The area's present boundaries with neighbouring Wiltshire communities have little historical precedent, therefore, and are based more on geographical and social reality, the natural barriers of Savernake Forest and the Avon-Bourne watershed, and the mushrooming of military Tidworth.

Warminster

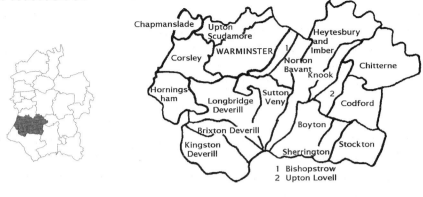

At Warminster the River Deverill turns east to become the River Wylye, and carves its exquisite but traffic-laden valley between the majestic southern spurs (Arn Hill, Battlesbury, and Scratchbury) of Salisbury Plain, and the wide unnamed block of chalkland along which runs the Great Ridge. Much of the community area is empty downland, either the rank grass of deserted Imber's ghosts in the heart of Salisbury Plain, or the rolling fields of Pertwood above Longbridge Deverill. But from Warminster westwards to the Somerset border greensand dominates, bringing unpredictability and large tracts of woodland to the scenery around Corsley and Horningsham. Here, too, straddling the county boundary, sits Longleat in its magnificent park.

Warminster has been a cloth and glove manufacturing centre, with a very important agricultural market. It was also a 'thoroughfare' town (now mercifully by-passed) along the road from Bath to Salisbury. Georgian prosperity is evident in its impressively long principal street, and it is still an important shopping centre. During the present century its economy and population have been boosted by the infantry barracks built between the town and the plain. The villages of the upper Wylye and Deverill valleys are typically small, compact, and desirable, and one of them – Heytesbury – was formerly a small town and Parliamentary borough. Chitterne, away from the valley and isolated on Salisbury Plain, shows us what might have become of its neighbour, Imber, had the army not confiscated it in 1943. Horningsham and Corsley display a very different settlement pattern. They lie within the area of the former Selwood Forest, and their dispersed hamlets and farms are typical of relict woodland.

The area has a larger than average population, but only a modest rise is projected to 2001, with little inward migration and relatively few new houses. Unemployment is above average for Wiltshire, with the second lowest proportion of qualified working males, and the second lowest incidence of car ownership.

Apart from Kingston Deverill, which was transferred from Mere RDC in 1934, this community is coterminous with the former Warminster RDC, which in turn was derived from an 1834 poor law union. The union followed most of the boundaries of two hundreds, Warminster and Heytesbury. Administratively, therefore, the community conforms very well to ancient divisions. The 1934 transfer of Kingston Deverill into this community was in tune with the topography of the area, since it brought the whole of the Deverill valley into the same unit of government. The community area also conforms fairly well to Warminster's historic sphere of influence (as seen, for example by the route map of village carriers, and the school catchment areas), except that some of its eastern parishes tend to look to Salisbury as their centre.

East Street, Warminster

Amesbury

AT THE HEART of this community area is the valley of the Salisbury or Christchurch Avon, which takes a meandering course southerly between the folds of Salisbury Plain, and – south of Amesbury – creates a masterpiece of riverbank scenery, the so-called Woodford valley. North of Amesbury the valley is wider and more severe, and violated here and there by military paraphernalia. A second, smaller, river converges on Salisbury, and serves the villages to the south-east of Amesbury. This is the Bourne, for much of the year dry or insignificant, but occasionally, like all winterbournes, metamorphosed into a torrent. The same is true of the Till, a minor tributary of the Wylye, which serves Tilshead, Orcheston, and Shrewton, high on Salisbury Plain. Away from the valleys and their agricultural hillsides, the whole area is chalk downland, empty apart from the military ubiquity.

Virtually all settlement in the area lies in the valleys, where villages and hamlets dot each riverbank every mile or so. The only exceptions, apart from lonely barns and sheilings, have occurred within the last century, with the creation of garrisons at Bulford and Larkhill, and a military camp at Westdown above Tilshead. Amesbury, too, has expanded from its historic nucleus beside the river, up the hillside eastwards to meet the defence research airfield at Boscombe Down. Shrewton, with nearly 2,000 inhabitants, is a large village, or rather a coalescence of several adjacent villages. The string of settlements along the Bourne valley is also quite populous. But the majority of people in the community area live in one of the three contiguous parishes at its heart, Amesbury, Bulford, or Durrington. Together they boast a population of around 20,000, more than half that of Salisbury. Of the three Amesbury is and has always been the urban centre, with a range of shops and services, whereas Durrington and Bulford are villages which have grown disproportionate suburbs since 1900. The Amesbury area exists in close symbiosis with

Salisbury to the south. Commuting into the city seems to be evenly matched by Salisbury residents heading north to employment in the military camps.

The area's population is greater than that of most Wiltshire communities, but is set to rise relatively little to 2001, and the number of new dwellings and the projected rate of inward migration are the lowest in the county. The existence of major sites for new housing and employment development may, however, lead to increased rates of change in the longer term. Average income and the incidence of car ownership are relatively high, and the unemployment rate the lowest in Wiltshire, despite a much smaller proportion of the workforce than average having qualifications.

Like Wilton and Downton, Salisbury's other satellite towns, Amesbury has never been powerful enough to extend much of a sphere of influence further than its immediate neighbours. It was the centre of a poor law union, however, and a rural district which adopted the same boundaries. With the exception of Winterbourne Stoke, lost to Wilton, these boundaries have been followed by the community area, which can therefore point to strong historical precedent as an administrative unit. Beyond this claim, easy road access to Amesbury from both the Shrewton and Cholderton areas gives this community area rather more coherence than topography and its ragged boundaries would otherwise suggest.

Salisbury Street, Amesbury.

Mere and Tisbury

AFTER MARLBOROUGH, Mere and Tisbury is the largest community in area, and also the second most thinly populated, with some of the emptiest and most appealing landscapes. Chalk downland dominates its northern and southern fringes, but sandwiched between is the valley of the River Nadder, generally known as the Vale of Wardour. Greensand gives variety and irregularity to the scenery, especially around the Knoyles and Donheads, while at Tisbury and Chilmark the river has cut through to the underlying limestones, which have been extensively quarried. Around Mere is flat clayland, the eastern limit of Dorset's Blackmore Vale, but moving westward to the county boundary greensand is encountered again, and this has permitted one of the triumphs of landscape modification, the gardens of Stourhead.

Mere itself is the only town in the area, but with a little over 2,000 inhabitants, it is the smallest centre of any of Wiltshire's communities. Tisbury is not far behind, and has an urban feel, although this is the result of Victorian expansion once the railway had arrived, rather than historical importance. In fact it supplanted nearby Hindon, a medieval planted town, as the minor administrative centre for the Vale of Wardour. None of the other villages is particularly large, and because of the varying geology there is no stereotype. The Donheads are diffuse, Semley has a large green, Chicklade and Zeals line a main road, Stourton and Hindon have been artificially planned. The pull of Salisbury is felt as one moves eastward through this area, although for immediate needs many residents turn to neighbouring small towns in Dorset or Somerset – Shaftesbury, Gillingham, or Wincanton.

Although the area's population is small, a relatively high rate of inward migration is projected to 2001, more than offsetting a local excess of deaths over births. Average incomes and unemployment are in the middle of the range, with a slightly higher than average proportion of the workforce having qualifications. Car ownership and long-distance commuting are also above average.

This community's area nearly corresponds to that of the Mere and Tisbury RDC, which existed between 1934 and 1974, and replaced two separate RDCs based on 1834 poor law unions. They in turn approximated to the ancient hundreds of Mere and Dunworth. The discrepancies between the pre-1974 RDC and the community area are Alvediston, which has sensibly been grouped with its neighbours in the Chalke valley under Wilton, and the intertwining settlements of Fovant and Sutton Mandeville, which have been brought into this area because of their proximity to Tisbury. The transfer of Kingston Deverill from Mere to Warminster in 1934 has already been noted. Nowhere in this area, as suggested above, has developed a significant sphere of influence, the attractions of neighbouring Dorset and Somerset places being felt as strongly as Mere, Tisbury, and Salisbury.

Wilton

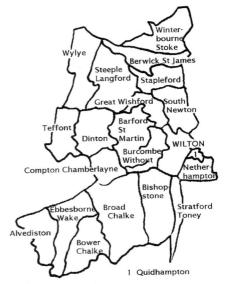

WILTON, PERHAPS SURPRISINGLY, has the lowest and most thinly spread population of any of the community areas. This is because it includes large tracts of chalk downland – to the north on Salisbury Plain, and to the south on Cranborne Chase – and also an extensive area of woodland where the chalk is mantled by flinty clay along the ridge between Wishford and Barford, known as Grovely. No fewer than four rivers serve this exclusively chalkland area: the Wylye and the Nadder, which meet at Wilton; the Till, which flows into the Wylye at Stapleford; and the Ebble or Chalke, which flows eastwards along the area's southern edge, to meet the Avon below Salisbury.

Wilton, which may have given the county its name, was a regional centre long before Salisbury existed, and remains one of the most rewarding of Wiltshire's small towns to explore. It has a market place with a weekly market, and a range of interesting shops, although it is a sad fact for its traders that, since at least the 14th century, most people have travelled through Wilton on their way to Salisbury. But it remains urban, with nearly 4,000 population, and is still not quite a suburb of the city next door. Apart from Wylye, formerly an oasis for travellers along the Exeter road, and Broad Chalke, at the centre of the Chalke valley, the villages of the community area have little significance beyond their own boundaries. As befits the chalklands they are tight-knit and strung regularly along their valleys. Several, including Teffont and Great Wishford, are admired for the beauty of their buildings and setting, and very few could not be described as attractive.

The area has a much higher than average proportion of qualified workers, but a low average income. Unemployment, long-distance commuting, new housing, and the projected rate of inward migration are all towards the middle of the range.

The boundaries of the community area conform quite well to those of a poor law union based on Wilton (its workhouse survives between the A36 railway bridges), which were adopted in 1894 for Wilton RDC. Between 1934 and 1974 this was combined with the area south-east of Salisbury to create Salisbury and Wilton RDC — so the present community puts back the clock to 1934 and earlier. The RDC boundaries were not quite identical, however, to those of the modern community. Alvediston, at the head of the Chalke valley, has been gained from Mere; and Winterbourne Stoke and Stratford Toney have been taken from Amesbury and Downton (former Salisbury RDC) respectively. Wilton, as suggested above, does not really have a commercial sphere of influence extending far beyond its own borders, but its school catchment area corresponds quite closely to the boundaries of its community.

Salisbury

SALISBURY'S COMMUNITY AREA is coterminous with the city itself, and so is easily the smallest but most densely populated of the nineteen. It sits in a valley at the confluence of the Avon, Nadder (augmented by the Wylye), and Bourne, and in the shadow of a prehistoric hillfort, Old Sarum, which was recolonized and refortified in the 11th century to become Wiltshire's cathedral city. Salisbury, or New Sarum as it is also known, was built around the new cathedral in the 13th century, and quickly supplanted the hilltop settlement to become a regional capital and one of the largest and most important towns in medieval England.

By the 17th century stagnation had deprived it of that distinction, but it has retained an effective hinterland embracing virtually the whole of south Wiltshire and adjacent parts of Dorset and Hampshire. Suburban expansion occurred in all directions from about 1820 onwards, embracing the historic villages of Fisherton, Harnham, and Bemerton, and extending northwards towards Old Sarum. As a service, educational, cultural and shopping centre, and a mecca for tourists, it probably needs no particular industrial base, but it has benefited greatly from the military presence on Salisbury Plain. It has also attracted the relocated headquarters of a number of national organizations, and its rail and road links have brought it within London commuting distance. It is justly famous, not only for its faultless cathedral, but also for the wealth of medieval buildings in its chequerboard of planned streets, and for its spectacularly large market place.

Salisbury is the most populous town in the new Wiltshire, although the total population of its community area is exceeded by that of Chippenham (which includes a rural hinterland). It yields only to Chippenham, too, in the projected rate of inward migration and new housing to 2001, and the predicted population rise over the same period is above the average. Its unemployment rate is exceeded only by Trowbridge, and the average income is very low, despite a high rate of qualifications among the male workforce. The incidence of car ownership is the lowest in Wiltshire, with a large proportion of the employed population working, as well as living, in the city. Many of these characteristics, of course, stem from Salisbury community area's unique position in being entirely urban, without a rural hinterland.

Since the community boundary reflects the limits of urban and suburban Salisbury itself, progressively enlarged as the city has grown, its validity is self-evident.

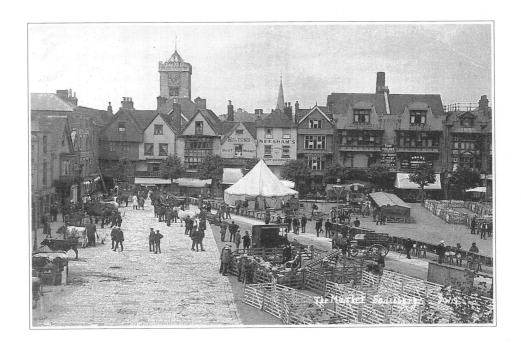

Downton

A TRIANGLE at the south-east corner of Wiltshire, the Downton community area is bordered on two of its sides by Hampshire. Except at Winterslow in the north, and along its western edge, in the Clearbury area and above Coombe Bissett, we find ourselves leaving the familiar chalk for the younger rocks – clays and heathland sands – of the Hampshire Basin. From Pepperbox Hill above Whiteparish the view is not only back towards Salisbury, but also into Hampshire's Test Valley. And when we stray south and east of Downton, into the woodlands of Redlynch and Nomansland, there is an unmistakeable sense of the New Forest. Between these Wiltshire and Hampshire aspects of the area the River Avon flows south from Salisbury to Downton, having gathered up the Bourne on the city outskirts and the Ebble at Bodenham.

In reality the Downton area, like the Wilton and Amesbury communities, is in thrall to Salisbury for many of its services and facilities, and it is most doubtful whether Winterslow or Laverstock residents would ever call on Downton to meet their needs in preference to Salisbury. Nevertheless, the parishes of Downton and Redlynch together muster a significant, if somewhat scattered, population of over 6,000, and Downton itself has a tradition as a small-scale town stretching back to the 13th century, when the Bishop of Winchester laid out the Borough adjacent to an existing village. Winterslow, Alderbury, Whiteparish, and Laverstock are large and straggling villages, all greatly augmented by recent suburban-style housing, but the area also includes a number of much smaller and more compact settlements, such as East Grimstead, Pitton, Odstock, and Nunton. Bournemouth and Southampton are in easy commuting distance of the Downton community, and the small Hampshire towns of Fordingbridge, Ringwood, and Romsey compete with Salisbury for its attention.

The area's population and population density, projected number of new dwellings, and rate of inward migration, are all within the middle of the range for Wiltshire communities, but the population is expected to rise relatively little to 2001. The Downton area records the highest average incomes in Wiltshire, the second highest incidence (after Malmesbury) of car ownership, and the third highest proportion of qualified male workers. Long-distance commuting is also well above average, and unemployment is relatively low.

With the minor exceptions of West Dean (formerly in Stockbridge union, Hampshire), Stratford Toney (now placed in Wilton community), and the encroachment of suburban Salisbury, the boundaries of Downton community area correspond to those of an 1834 poor law union based on Alderbury, which became Salisbury RDC in 1894. Between 1934 and 1974 this was combined with Wilton RDC, but the modern community has restored the earlier administrative tradition.

APPENDIX: COMMUNITY MATRIX

	Mal	Woo	Chp	Cor	Cal	Mar	Brd	Mel	Tro	Wes	Dev	Pew	Tid	War	Ame	Mer	Wil	Sal	Dow
Total Population	7	15	19	9	10	11	4	12	17	5	16	2	6	13	14	3	1	18	8
Density of Population	5	12	15	14	11	4	16	17	18	13	10	3	8	6	9	2	1	19	7
Area	14	10	8	6	7	19	2	3	5	4	13	11	9	17	15	18	16	1	12
Births 1991-2001	6	15	19	9	10	8	3	11	18	7	14	4	13	12	16	1	2	17	5
Deaths 1991-2001	6	13	17	9	8	11	7	14	18	4	16	2	1	15	12	5	3	19	10
Net Migration in 1991-2001	9	3	19	6	15	11	5	12	17	13	16	8	2	4	1	14	10	18	7
Population Increase 1991-2001	11	6	19	7	18	10	1	9	17	14	16	12	15	3	5	8	4	13	2
New Dwellings 1991-2001	9	3	19	6	15	11	5	12	17	13	16	8	2	4	1	14	10	18	7
Unemployment Rate 1997	2	4	10	12	14	7	16	3	19	17	13	5	15	11	8	8	9	18	6
Average Income 1991	18	17	12	9	11	15	16	1	4	7	8	14	6	2	13	10	5	3	19
Qualified Males %, 1991	16	7	12	14	9	18	19	4	8	5	6	10	1	2	3	11	15	13	17
Qualified Females %, 1991	7	4	1	19	2	9	12	18	6	10	15	11	14	17	1	13	16	18	8
Cars per Household, 1991	19	17	4	7	8	16	13	9	5	6	10	15	3	2	11	14	12	1	18
Commuting less than 5km, 1991	2	3	15	8	11	9	12	14	18	13	16	5	1	17	6	10	7	19	4
Commuting 20km or more, 1991	18	5	14	4	13	17	3	2	1	7	10	19	11	16	8	12	9	6	15

This matrix acts as a league table for comparing various social and demographic attributes of the nineteen community areas. Each row describes an attribute, and each column a community area. The figures represent each community's ranking, the lowest, fewest, or smallest being denoted by 1, the highest, most, or largest denoted by 19. The source of all data for constructing this table is the Community Area Profiles issued by Wiltshire County Council, Environmental Services Divison (see Further Reading below). It should be emphasized that many of the figures are based on projections to 2001 which may well change. Many of the comments made about the community areas in Chapter 3 have been derived from this table.

4 Belonging in a Community

Introduction

IF YOU HAVE ARRIVED at this point, Chapter 4, in the conventional way via Chapters 1, 2, and 3, you will by now have a good idea of the complexities involved in the notion of natural communities and how they have evolved. If you live in Wiltshire, Chapter 3 will have given you an opportunity to measure your own impression of the particular community in which you live against that imposed upon it by this book. Your image may differ from mine, and that of the Wiltshire local authorities, and we shall never all reach a consensus about where boundaries should be drawn between communities. We all live different lives and see our world in different ways.

But we can perhaps all agree, and public opinion research confirms, that most people identify with some kind of community. This chimerical notion of 'community' exists in people's minds and, however defined, it must include decision-making about matters of common concern. It follows that local democracy will work best when it is attuned to the communities with which people identify.

Background

THE CRUCIBLE of democracy, two-and-a-half millennia ago, was ancient Greece, a confederation of autonomous city-states, very similar in nature and scale to the communities of town and surrounding countryside with which this book is grappling. Everyone could become involved in the decision-making process, by attending public meetings, electing representatives and leaders, and casting votes to resolve important issues. Some of the democratic provisions of ancient Athens might not now be acceptable to local politicians. Ostracism, for example, was a mechanism whereby an unpopular demagogue could be removed from office and sent into exile by a simple referendum. Nevertheless, good local government, organized in a way sympathetic to the needs of communities, offers a much closer approximation to the original Greek ideal of democracy than do regional assemblies and national parliaments.

During the 1980s the pendulum of political ideology, as with hindsight we now realize, swung towards individual rights and liberties at the expense of collective responsibility, and private enterprise at the expense of public ownership. Many services became the responsibility of non-elected organizations, 'quangos', and public perception of local government, in some quarters, was that it was becoming aloof, monolithic, and distanced from the day-to-day needs of its citizens.

By 1990 this pendulum had begun its return, as county and district councils recognized, not only that they must become more responsive to the local communities which elected and helped to pay for them, but also that, amid the plethora of other service-providers, they might have a co-ordinating role to play. Bedfordshire County Council, for instance, established a policy commitment to devolve and decentralize in 1989, and appointed a 'decentralization officer' to oversee the process. A group of academics and local government executives established a Communitarian Forum, committed to building democratic communities which, in their words, they saw as, 'a sustainable alternative to the destructive individualism which has become the predominant ideology in this country for so long'.

The importance of the notion of communities and community development as a key approach to the local government of the future was gaining ground by the time of the 1992 Local Government Act, which gave the reviewing commission its terms of reference. These included recommending, 'such structural, boundary or electoral changes as may appear to it desirable having regard to the need to reflect the identities and interests of local communities...'. Community identity came under the spotlight, and a debate ensued about what it meant, its potential value to local governance, and how (if at all) it could be defined. The Association of District Councils, perhaps mindful of the original Greek model, suggested that, 'bonding local authority areas more strongly to the communities they represent and serve... is what local democracy should be all about'.

Progress and Intentions

ONE OUTCOME of the Local Government Review which created the new Wiltshire has been to place community identity and community focus high on the agenda for the development of local services. The commitment is embodied in Wiltshire County Council's emerging corporate strategy, for 1998-2002, which contains an undertaking to pursue its goals in partnership with communities and other organizations, so that the Council focuses on communities' needs and takes into account their views; Council services reflect users' needs; and people are more involved in planning and reviewing the Council's work. These aims are to be achieved: by working with local people and organizations to tackle local priorities; by greater collaboration between services, and with District and Local Councils and other agencies; by planning and organizing Council services as close to the user as possible, and involving service users more; and by improving consultation and communication with the public.

These intentions replace a previous, briefer strategic goal directed along similar lines, 'to extend the client and community focus of the County Council and its services to give individual communities and major stakeholders in Wiltshire a greater sense of involvement in the Council's work, by empowering clients and communities, and developing the planning of community services across the boundaries of departments at county and local level'.

As explained in the introduction, the Local Government Review drew attention to the importance of 'natural' communities, and subsequent policies and goals have emerged from work undertaken for that review. This included a MORI survey of community identity in Wiltshire, undertaken in November and December 1993, which found a clear hierarchy: a strong sense of belonging was most widespread towards the smallest areas, and least widespread towards the largest. Thus 78% identified strongly with their neighbourhood or village, 73% with their town or nearest town, 53% with their district or borough area, and 48% with the county area.

By analysing various other factors, such as commuting patterns, school and shopping catchment areas, administrative and postal boundaries, and by consulting parish and town councils, a provisional map of community boundaries was drawn up, and these were modified in the light of the historical considerations described in Chapter 3 of this book. The resulting division into nineteen community areas was presented to the Local Government Commission, and has provided a key organizing principle for county and district council services. It has been built on in various ways, not only by local government, but also by other service providers working in partnership. Progress, to the beginning of 1998, has been as follows:

Area Teams: In order to enhance the delivery of the highways service, the County's new Environmental Services Department has set up eight small locally-based highway teams. The area covered by each team consists of groupings of the community areas, all contained within existing District Council boundaries. Each area surveyor is expected to build close working relationships with local County and District members and with parish councils in their area. There are a number of examples where District Councils have used community areas or combinations of them, as a basis for administrative and service delivery structures.

Passenger Transport: A project to look comprehensively at passenger transport in the Devizes community area formed part of the County Council's bid to become one of the Government's 'Best Value' pilot authorities. The bid narrowly failed, but the County Council is still committed to the project, which will be undertaken as part of a wider process to develop an integrated transport strategy for the area, in partnership with Kennet District Council, local town and parish councils, and other interested organizations.

Strategic Planning and Statistical Information: Community areas have been adopted as the basic building blocks for analytical work to inform the development of the Structure Plan, superseding the former use of larger structure plan sectors. Relevant models and documents such as the population forecasting model, and the Rural Facilities Survey report are being based on the community areas.

Statistical profiles have been prepared for each of the community areas, and these will be revised and expanded in 1998.

Social Services: In April 1997 Social Services reorganised its Adult Care and Children and Families fieldwork teams based on groupings of whole community areas. These fieldwork teams, with only one exception, rest within District Council boundaries. As a result, Social Services is better able to develop partnerships at the local level with individuals and communities and to establish stronger working relationships with other agencies. Resource allocation systems for these fieldwork teams have also been developed based on the distinctive social characteristics of each community area.

Social Services is also working at the community area level with service users, carers, local statutory and voluntary sector providers, GPs and primary care teams, and other community groups to develop local community care plans for fieldwork team areas.

Social Services has also sought a greater local focus, and better integration with the Health Service, by working closely with GP practices, and has developed models of joint working which have been nationally recognised.

Education and Libraries: As they were devised using secondary school catchment areas as a key factor, the community areas were already a fundamental unit of the department's work with respect to schools.

An initiative is being developed between the Local Education Authority and schools to promote more effective links between schools and their local communities. It draws on a range of existing good practice in the county and will enhance and support this work. The outcomes sought by the partners in this initiative are several: more responsible, confident and competent young people / citizens; agencies like the local authorities, police and the health service better connected to young people and schools; schools better connected with their local communities; and local communities able to tap into the school as a learning and leisure resource.

The Youth Service has adopted the community areas as a basis for its local organization, and is seeking to establish youth forums to inform its work in specific areas.

The Library Service is currently replacing its computer system, and it is planned that the new system will be able to search and retrieve information from its community information database on a community area basis, as well as by other categories of search. The Local Studies and

County Records services can both reinforce the community area approach by providing a historical perspective to community issues and debates.

Information Points and Area Offices: The County Council in partnership with the four District Councils, and with local town and parish councils, has piloted the idea of joint local information points to deliver council and community information to particular community areas. The pilots have been located at Calne, Melksham, Marlborough and Mere.

This same partnership approach has informed North Wiltshire District Council's establishment of an area office to act as a focal point within each of its community areas. These offices will be places where the public can readily address problems, seek information or simply have the opportunity to discuss their concerns with an information officer, supported by appropriate information technology. Offices have already been established in Malmesbury and Wootton Bassett (where the service is called Cascade), and others will follow during 1998.

Salisbury District Council is also currently examining the potential of opening further information points in addition to Mere in the other community areas in the district.

District Council Area Committees: Salisbury District Council has recently introduced a system of multi-functional area committees throughout the district, following a one year's pilot in the Amesbury community area. The four area committees are based on community areas, or combinations of community areas. West Wiltshire District Council has created three area committees from the five community areas that cover the district. North Wiltshire District Council is committed to developing an area committee model in readiness for implementation in May 1999.

Both the Salisbury and West Wiltshire area committees have executive powers only for District Council services, but encourage attendance and involvement by local county, town and parish councillors, as well as the public, hence improving the co-ordination between the tiers of local government and providing a focus for local community participation and debate. The area committees meet at various locations within their areas, and take decision-making closer to the communities they serve.

Area Forums: Area Forums composed of all the County and District Councillors for a community area, and representatives of each of the town and parish councils, have been piloted in the Malmesbury and Devizes community areas. The pilots have no executive powers, but can provide a focus for the identification of local priority issues, and hence promote and inform local joint working towards common goals. Following a recent review it was agreed that the Devizes pilot would be extended for a further year. The forum meets quarterly.

Health Authority: The Health Authority has used the community area approach as the basis for its 'fair shares' investment strategy, aiming to spend a fair share of its financial allocation from the Government on the different communities, using measures of the health needs of the community area populations.

The Health Authority has also used the community area approach to involve local people and organizations, working with health professionals, to prepare local health plans for a number of the areas. This work is continuing.

Recently the Government has published a White Paper heralding changes in health service organization which will ensure that this early work by the Health Authority will be built upon. Most health service investment in future will be decided by Primary Care Groups - local groups of general practitioners and other health care professionals, with local government participation. Primary Care Groups will have a powerful influence over local health services. There are likely to be at least four groups in Wiltshire.

The Health Authority has formed 'healthy alliances' with local government across Wiltshire, to work together to improve the health of local people. The Government's recent Green Paper, 'Our Healthier Nation', underlines the message that environmental, social and economic factors play a large part in causing inequalities in health. The importance of local organizations working together at a local level to reduce these inequalities will be reflected in the future of community partnerships.

Economic Development: There are a number of initiatives in the county aimed at regenerating Wiltshire's town centres, and several towns have appointed town centre managers. The County Council's Strategy and Regeneration Group has developed, in association with the Urban and Economic Development Group (URBED), and a group of local people with experience of community-led initiatives, a practical guide to revitalising Wiltshire's towns and villages.

Community Safety: The Crime and Disorder Bill will require the Police, and the County and District Councils, to set up, where they do not already exist, community safety partnerships based on District Council areas. These partnerships would seek to develop projects at the local community area level.

Local Meetings with Staff: As part of the setting up of the new Wiltshire County Council following Local Government Reorganization in April 1997, the Chief Executive arranged meetings with local county staff in each of the nineteen community areas. At the same time as explaining the outlook of the new Council, the opportunity was taken of asking staff to identify what were the distinctive features of each community area, and what they thought were the key issues each area faced.

Boundary Reviews: The community areas have been used as a factor in a number of boundary reviews, including the current reviews of district electoral wards, and of magistrates' petty sessional divisions. The Wiltshire Association of Local Councils (WALC) which represents the collective interests of town and parish councils, elects its Executive Committee using the community areas as electoral areas.

An Overall Framework: Since mid-1997 the responsibility for setting the overall framework for improvements to the way the three tiers of local government work together in Wiltshire has rested with the Wiltshire branch of the Local Government Association. In September 1997 this body agreed a strategic statement:

> Wiltshire local authorities in the foreseeable future face increasing demands on services without equivalent increases in resources.
> Wiltshire local authorities in the future wish to involve Wiltshire communities to a greater extent and to have more consultation and local participation.
> Local Government in the future wishes to put more emphasis on developing policies that seek to add value through working together by implementing effective prevention strategies and to give priority to these issues.

Working in partnership, particularly between the three tiers of local government, is of key importance. The philosophy of the partnership must be embraced by all (councillors and officers), and in committing themselves to partnership each of the constituent councils recognises that:
–   The purpose of local partnerships is to enable each partner to add value.
–   Effective partnership involves give and take by all sides.

The Wiltshire Local Government Association commended the following principles to the constituent authorities as a basis for developing partnership arrangements. All Councils will:
–   Take action at the most 'local' level possible.
–   Seek common boundaries for working together in localities.
–   Favour simplicity over complexity when working together.
–   Value local diversity.
–   Fit in with existing structures, if possible.
–   Identify community needs together, and (wherever relevant) commission services jointly.
–   Go beyond agreements into joint action and implementation.
–   Provide information for the public on a joint basis.
–   Open up organizations to each other's staff — by secondments, joint training, joint appointment processes, joint reviews.
–   Examine opportunities for combining services.

In assessing the value of partnership working, the Wiltshire Local Government Association commended to its constituent authorities the following tests:
–   Would the partnership improve services?
–   Would it reduce overall expenditure levels?
–   Would it help to deliver more community focused services or activities?

It is essential that working in partnership adds value.

Postscript

WHEN DESCRIBING current concerns and immediate intentions any book renders itself out of date as soon as it is published, if not before. My main purpose has been to place the issues facing today's local government into some kind of historical perspective. And in this area I hope that my book may have a somewhat longer shelf life. The suggestion that one should learn from the 'lessons of history' is often repeated but seldom, in my experience, taken very seriously. Most working local historians, in fact, probably never consider that the material which they work with every day could have a direct bearing on the way decisions affecting us all are made now. It was a surprise and honour for me, therefore, to be asked in 1993 to bring local history into the arena of the Local Government Review, and gratifying that a much amended (in fact, largely rewritten) version of my report is now to be given wider exposure through publication.

I should like to pay tribute to the skill and forbearance of three Wiltshire County Council officers: David Maynard, who first suggested that the original report be commissioned; David Landeryou, who has read and commented on my use of statistical information (much of which he collected and compiled); and John Feane, who proposed that my report be published in this form. I should also like to acknowledge Roger Jones, of Ex Libris Press, my long-suffering publisher; and the staff of the County Local Studies Library, Trowbridge, for research facilities, as well as for permitting use of the historic photographs included in Chapter 3.

FURTHER READING

THIS BOOK is based on research conducted for my unpublished report, *The History of Wiltshire and its Communities* (1993), which includes a full bibliography of all sources consulted. Only the most significant works are included in the following suggestions for further reading. They are grouped into three sections: books and articles relevant to the history of Wiltshire's administration and boundaries (corresponding to Chapter 1); sources of statistical and current policy information (Chapters 2 and 4); and a selection of historical works relating to the principal places in each community (Chapter 3). Relevant to all three sections are articles in the *Victoria County History of Wiltshire*, volumes 1-15, and these are cited simply as VCH, followed by the volume number.

Wiltshire's Administration and Boundaries

Barron, R.S., 1976, *The geology of Wiltshire: a field guide*
Bonney, Desmond J., 1972, 'Early boundaries in Wessex', *Archaeology and the landscape*, ed. P.J. Fowler, pp.168-86
Bracey, H.E., 1952, *Social provision in rural Wiltshire*
Chisholm, Michael, 1979, *Rural settlement and land use: an essay in location*
Fitzmaurice, Lord, and Bown, W.L., 1920, *The boundaries of the administrative county of Wilts*
Grant, Eric, 1986, *Central places, archaeology and history*
Harloe, Michael, 1975, *Swindon, a town in transition: a study in urban development and overspill policy*
Haslam, Jeremy, 1984, *Anglo-Saxon towns in southern England*
Hudson, Kenneth, 1967, *An awkward size for a town: a study of Swindon at the 100,000 mark*
Loyn, H.R., 1984, *The governance of Anglo-Saxon England, 500-1087*
Rogers, K.H., 1976, *Wiltshire and Somerset woollen mills*
Underdown, David, 1985, *Revel, riot and rebellion: popular politics and culture in England 1603-1660*
VCH vols. 2, 4, 5
Yorke, Barbara, 1995, *Wessex in the early middle ages*

Statistics and Policy

[Note: enquiries about WCC statistical documents should be directed to David Landeryou (01225-713469), and about policy documents to David Maynard (01225-713118)]
Ball, Rick, and Stobart, Jon, 1996, 'Community identity and the local government review', *Local Government Studies*, vol.22, pp.113-26
Tam, Henry, 1996, 'Communitarianism and citizens empowerment', *Local Government Policy Making*, vol.22, pp.52-6
Tizard, John N., and Holman, Kay, 1995, 'Communities, governance and local democracy: roles and relationships', *Local Government Policy Making*, vol.21, pp.3-8
VCH vol.4
Wiltshire County Council, 1974, *Wiltshire basic data* [Social Services Department]
Wiltshire County Council, 1978, *South Wiltshire structure plan: report of survey*
Wiltshire County Council, 1979a, *North East Wiltshire structure plan: report of survey*
Wiltshire County Council, 1979b, *Western Wiltshire structure plan: report of survey*

Wiltshire County Council, 1993, *County trends, 1981-2002* [1998 edition in preparation]
Wiltshire County Council, 1994, *Review of local government in Wiltshire: submission by the County Council to the Local Government Commission*, 2 parts
Wiltshire County Council, 1996, *Wiltshire community areas: 1991 census profiles*
Wiltshire County Council, 1997a, *Creating the new Wiltshire: an opportunity to discuss the future* [preliminary statistical profiles of each community area]
Wiltshire County Council, 1997b, *Population estimates: parishes, wards and towns, 1996*
Wiltshire County Council, 1997c, *Population projections 2001 and 2011*
Wiltshire County Council, 1997d, *Service plan, 1998/9 - 2000/2001*
Wiltshire County Council, 1997e, *Rural facilities survey*
Wiltshire County Council, 1998, *Corporate strategy, 1998-2002*

Histories of Specific Places

Malmesbury: VCH vol.14 covers Malmesbury itself and most of the community area.
Wootton Bassett: VCH vol.9 covers Wootton Bassett itself and much of the community area. For Cricklade see Holmes, Diana, 1993, *Cricklade*
Chippenham: Chamberlain, J.A., 1976, *Chippenham*. Much tourist literature about Castle Combe.
Corsham: No modern history of Corsham; Box and Colerne have recent locally-produced histories, by Claire Higgens, and the Colerne History Group respectively. Many tourist guides to Lacock.
Calne: No modern history of Calne: see Marsh, A.E.W., 1904, *History of the borough and town of Calne*; for Cherhill: Blackford, J.H., 1941, *The manor and village of Cherhill*.
Marlborough: Most of the community area, including Marlborough itself, is covered in VCH vol.12.
Bradford on Avon: For Bradford itself see Fassnidge, H., 1993, *Bradford on Avon past and present*; 2nd ed.; and Dobson, Margaret, 1997, *Bradford Voices*. Most of the area is covered in VCH vol.7.
Melksham: VCH vol.7 covers the whole community area.
Trowbridge: VCH vols.7 and 8 cover the whole community area. See also histories of Trowbridge itself by K.H. Rogers, 1984 and 1994.
Westbury: VCH vol.8 covers the whole community area.
Devizes: For Devizes itself see Haycock, Lorna, 1993, *Devizes: history and guide*; and Bradby, Edward, 1985, *The book of Devizes*. VCH vols.7 and 10 cover the whole area (Devizes is in vol.10).
Pewsey: Most of the community area is covered in VCH vols.10 and 11. Pewsey itself, and its eastern neighbours, will be included in VCH vol.16 (1999). See also Chandler, John, 1991, *The Vale of Pewsey*.
Tidworth: Part of the community area is covered in VCH vols.11 and 15. See also Croman, D.J., 1991, *A history of Tidworth and Tedworth House*; and Dixon, Winifred, 1994, *A history of Ludgershall*.
Warminster: Part of the community area (including Warminster itself) is covered in VCH vol.8; and Stockton is in VCH vol.11.
Amesbury: VCH vol.15 covers most of the community area, including Amesbury – for which see also, Chandler, John, and Goodhugh, Peter, 1989, *Amesbury: history and description of a south Wiltshire town*; 2nd ed. Woodford and Wilsford are in VCH vol.6. Books on Stonehenge are legion.
Mere: Much of the community area (although not Mere itself) is covered in VCH vols.11 and 13. For Mere see Johnson, N.E.E. and others, 1958, *The story of Mere*.
Wilton: Wilton itself is covered in VCH vol.6, and other parts of the area are scattered in vols.8, 11, 13, and 15.
Salisbury: VCH vol.6 is the standard work. The most recent histories are by John Chandler, 1983 and 1992.
Downton: Downton and Redlynch are covered in VCH vol.11. Local studies exist for some villages, notably Pitton and Farley, by Michael Parsons.

INDEX

EXPLORING HISTORIC WILTSHIRE: Volumes 1 & 2

This major new work by Ken Watts focuses on twelve of the finest rural landscapes in Wiltshire.

Volume 1 deals with the north of the county and includes Ridgeway Country; The Central Marlborough Downs; Wansdyke; Grigson Country; Calstone, Oldbury and Roundway Down; The Vale of Pewsey.

Volume 2 covers the south of the county to include Chute Causeway; The Wylye Valley; Wiltshire Selwood & White Sheet Downs; Great Ridge & Grovely Woods; The South Wiltshire Ridgeways; South-East Wiltshire.

Each book contains 176 pages and is illustrated throughout with a mixture of black and white photographs, sketch maps and line drawings.
Both are priced at £7.95

THE PROSPECT OF WILTSHIRE

Words by John Chandler; pictures by Jim Lowe; maps by Karen Pigott
The first and only full-colour book dedicated to the beauties of this special county.

112 pages; full colour photographs and maps throughout; Price £14.95

BRADFORD VOICES

A Study of Bradford on Avon through the Twentieth Century
by Margaret Dobson
'…a remarkable social history. It is scholarly and reliable, detailed but never dull, and it flows seamlessly and fairly, through all the events and issues of Bradford's recent past, bringing them (and us) firmly into the present.'
256 pages; illustrated throughout; Price £9.95

PEDLARS PACK by John Chandler
1 A BATH ASSORTMENT
2 A SALISBURY ASSORTMENT

Small format books on English towns, each Pedlar's Pack volume is a mini-anthology and a perfect keepsake of particular places.
Each is 80 pages, illustrated with line drawings and priced at £3.95